MICHAEL HEATLEY

C000048833

IN THEIR OWN WORDS

Manic Street Preachers

MANIC STREET PREACHERS... IN THEIR OWN WORDS

Exclusive distributors:

Book Sales Limited
8-9 Frith Street, London W1V 5TZ, UK

Music Sales Corporation
257 Park Avenue South, New York, NY 10010, USA

Music Sales Pty Limited
120 Rothschild Avenue, Rosebery, NSW 2018, Australia

Exclusive distributors to the music trade only:

Music Sales Limited
8-9 Frith Street, London W1V 5TZ, UK

ISBN 0.7119.6906.X
Order No. OP48068

Compilation and introduction by Michael Heatley
Edited by Robert Dimery

Designed by Hilite Design & Reprographics Ltd

Picture research by Nikki Russell, Omnibus Press

All photographs by Aki/Retna:43;Piers Allardyce/SIN:12; Franck
Camhi/Retna:92; John Cheeves/ SIN:80,83; Joe
Dilworth/SIN:63,66/67; Steve Double: f/c bottom, 3,34,52,60/61,
86,89,94,95; Chris Floyd/Retna:7; Martin
Goodacre/SIN:19,30,31,70,72,82; Liane Hentcher/SIN:
22/23,40/41; LFI: b/c,2,4,5,9,13,14,18,24,26,27,28,29,
36,39,44,47,48,49,51,58,68,73,74,76,78,85,91; Tony
Mottram/Retna: 6; Tim Paton/SIN: 20,62; Ed Sirrs/Retna:16; Paul
Slattery /Retna: f/c top,64; Roy Tee/SIN: 54,56; Ian T.Tilton/SIN:
10; Niels Van Iperen/Retna: 50; Pete Walsh/Retna: 32.

Every effort has been made to trace the copyright holders of the
photographs in this book but one or two were unreachable. We
would be grateful if the photographers concerned would contact
us.

Printed in Great Britain by
Page Bros Ltd, Norwich, Norfolk

Visit Omnibus Press at
http://www.musicsales.co.uk

*Many thanks to Charlotte Worthington, an avid
Manics fan, for invaluable additional research.*

OMNIBUS PRESS

MANIC STREET PREACHERS...IN THEIR OWN WORDS

Think of Wales, the famed Land of Song, and a few years ago you'd probably have conjured up images of Shirley Bassey, Tom Jones, Harry Secombe and male voice choirs. Those with long and less cliché-ridden imaginations might have spotlighted Man, those indefatigable psychedelic pioneers who've been on the road for 30 years, Andy Fairweather Low or even Welsh-language singer-songwriter Meic Stevens.

Now, in the final years of the millenium, the charts and stages of Britain fairly resound to the sounds of the Principality. Catatonia, 60ft Dolls, Super Furry Animals – the roll of honour goes on. And in the vanguard of this new movement are the Manic Street Preachers, the undisputed Crown Princes of Wales.

The *Rough Guide To Rock* describes the Manics as first and foremost a gang who formed in 1986 on the tenth anniversary of the Sex Pistols. This isn't a history lesson, but that's a handy image to keep in mind as we trawl through a decade of public utterances from the foursome. That foursome is now, of course, a threesome after the mysterious disappearance of rhythm guitarist Richey James Edwards. The last to join (in 1989, replacing the quaintly named Flicker after their first DIY single 'Suicide Alley'), he was the first to leave, checking out of his hotel on 1 February 1995 on the eve of an American tour. He hasn't been seen since.

The Manics carried on, just as they had when Richey had been temporarily institutionalised following spells of depression. His musical input was debatable – cynics claimed his guitar was turned down on stage – but his contribution to songwriting, image and attitude was undeniable

Ironically, the band's first release as a three-piece, *Everything Must Go* (with five lyrics from Richey), was the one that catapulted them into the big league. Yet, as will become apparent as you leaf through these quotes, they've never lost that four-square gang mentality – us against the world. Which side are *you* on? Read... then decide.

A Welsh Childhood

People always ask, 'Were you outsiders at school, were you really weird?'. No, we just stayed in our bedrooms and watched TV. We never had anything else to do. We made no effort to make other friends because we felt so happy with each other.
Richey (1992)

We were never particularly victimised for being weird, because nobody ever saw us.
Nicky (1994)

If you built a museum to represent Blackwood, all you could put in it would be shit. We used to meet by this opening called Pen-Y-Fan. It was built when the mines closed but now the water has turned green and slimy. They put 2,000 fish in it, but they died. There's a whirlpool in the middle where about two people die every year.
Nicky (1994)

A long terraced street. Steps down into the valley. Football field. Swimming pool. Then to the left was a big disused slag heap with trees growing on it. We played there, everything happened there – Bonfire Night, Hallowe'en, a lot of people lost their virginity there. If there was a fight, it happened on that slag heap. It's gone now, levelled. When I go back, what strikes me is there's less places for people to hide. Hide and just be innocent. Lose their innocence, too.
James (1996)

Me and Richey used to play football for a cup my dad found on a rubbish tip. It was a crown-green bowls cup, but we ran down the street with it when we won anyway. Richey was on my team (Woodfield Side) and one day James brought Sean along to play for Pont.
Nicky (1996)

We're the sad victims of 20th-century culture. The cinema in our town, which is the poorest and most boring town in the country, closed down when we were eight, so what do you do? You go out and get pissed and have fights, or you stay in and get on with your boredom. We were happier to go along with the boredom.
Richey (1992)

The most exciting thing was sitting around reading the rock press. When *New Musical Express* said things like Eddie Cochran is an anarchist, we went 'yeah'. We fell for all that because our lives were really boring.
Richey (1992)

Nick tried joyriding once. He stole a car when he was 17. He didn't drive it into a shop. He just sort of rolled down the street, didn't get very far. He was a stunted joyrider. I think he fell asleep, drunk, at the wheel.
Richey (1991)

Depression is just our natural mood. Where we come from, there's a natural melancholy in the air. Everybody, ever since you could comprehend it, felt pretty much defeated. You've got the ruins of heavy industry all around you, you see your parents' generation all out of work, nothing to do, being forced into the indignity of going on 'courses of relevance'.
Richey (1994)

We grew up very early. By the time I was 16 I'd read and studied the complete works of Philip Larkin, Shakespeare, all the Beat generation, every film. I find it unbelievable, the intensity of us as people and as a band.
Nicky (1994)

When we were growing up, Richey's nickname was Teddy Edwards, after the cartoon character, because he was so cuddly. We just generally had a blissful childhood, in the sense of being free. Especially Richey, up until he was about 16, when he just hit the wall.
Nicky (1996)

Maybe that's what fucked us up, not that we had bad childhoods, but that our childhoods were too good. That sense of freedom – we weren't just reading books or watching films, experiencing second-hand culture, we were building a dam, messing around in dirt, things like that which, looking back, seem much more worthwhile.
Nicky (1994)

Up to the age of 13 I was ecstatically happy. People treated me very well, my dog was beautiful, I lived with my Nan and she was beautiful. School's nothing – you go there, come back and just play football in the fields. Then I moved from my Nan's and started a comprehensive school and everything started going wrong. In my 20s, there's nothing that's been that spectacular since.
Richey (1994)

I don't think we could have done this if we hadn't grown up in a shithole where the only way to escape was to create your own reality.
Nicky (1992)

I wanted to be someone like Napoleon. Then I discovered music – or the Clash to be more precise, and that was it. My destiny was determined.
James (1991)

Comprehensive school was the most depressing time for all of us. They either write you off or fit you in. If you're not academically gifted, it's 'fuck you'. If you are, it's, 'the banks are coming next week for a talk, and we think you should go.'
Richey (1992)

I enjoyed A Levels because you had a certain freedom to write what you liked, and also you had teachers who wanted to teach you, whereas at university all the lecturers really want to do is write books. They haven't the first idea how to teach and they don't care about making the subject interesting. They just indulge themselves.
Nicky (1994)

Most people look back on their childhoods with more fondness than their early twenties or their teenage years which are pretty horrendous. As a child, you put your head on the pillow and fall asleep with no worries. From being a teenager onwards it's pretty rare that you don't end up staying awake half the night thinking about bullshit.
Richey

A lot of going to university was three more years of not having to decide what to do with my life. I've literally never done a day's work in my life, not even a paper round, so I couldn't handle going to work in an office.
Nicky (1994)

I was much more outwardly nervous then. I always had a kind of quiet arrogance, and slight bitterness against the world, but I didn't have the guts to do anything about it.
Nicky (1994)

GENERATION TE
NATWEST-BAR
METHADONE 1
YOU LOVE US
FACELESS
STRIP IT DOW
CRUCIFIX KIS
SORROW 16
MOTOWN JU
TENNESSEE
REPEAT

Early/Indie Years

We came together around Nick. I was Baldrick to his Blackadder. More than anything he talked about being great, being legends. Nick reckoned he would be a great sportsman, a great politician. We started on the basis of those delusions of grandeur.
James (1996)

A big moment was on the tenth anniversary of punk. The Clash were on a compilation of that Tony Wilson programme *So It Goes*, doing 'Garageland' and 'What's My Name'. That was the catalyst to us forming a band. We thought we could look like that, walk it like that. Although we couldn't play...
Nicky (1996)

We started at a time when rock'n'roll was dead over here. The UK was in the grip of dance, rap and the acid house thing. All that Manchester sound stuff that sounded so contrived... The only real rock'n'roll was coming out of America. We were consciously reacting against all that. Our friends laughed at us because they said there was no audience for us. But we felt we had to do something to bring back rock'n'roll, so that's how the Manic Street Preachers came about.
Richey (1992)

Nick's first lyric was called 'Aftermath' – a real doggerel diatribe against Margaret Thatcher. The (miners') strike was all around us and it was on TV every day for a year. When the Yorkshire miners started turncoating, I'd find myself shouting at the telly: 'scab, scab'. But when it was over we didn't want to be these Welsh, working-class gangsters singing, 'We lost, we lost, but we're still standing'. We didn't believe in glorious losers.
James (1996)

We looked down on anyone outside the circle of the four of us. We didn't feel a generation gap with people who were older than us, we felt one with people of the same age. I think that's why we used sloganeering language a lot. We thought that was all they understood and deserved.
James (1996)

It was absolutely everything to me. My idea was about true, natural talent. Something you're born with. We always knew the band was going to work, and that it was just down to us to make it happen.
Sean (1996)

We had this evangelical desire to start the revolution and be absolutely fucking massive. It didn't just mean getting a record deal. It was all-conquering, psycho, egotistical.
Nicky (1996)

At the start I was personally on a mission to separate ourselves from everyone, even music that I liked. It's my bad trait.
Nicky (1996)

I used to commute in on the train. Regular work. Drum until six and then go home. It was like a little office job.
Sean (1996)

When we started we used to go into NatWest, all the banks, and try to get a loan. We'd tell them, 'this country is dead musically, there's got to be room for an exciting rock band.' We'd show them the *New Musical Express*; 'look at that, anything good in there? Now look at us, we're really exciting'. We told them we were going to be this really massive rock'n'roll band. They couldn't see it.
Richey (1991)

Once we got set our minds what we were doing, we didn't play a single gig in Blackwood. It was straight to London and scrounging money to get on the

pay-to-play circuit. You know, £50 for 15 minutes. Next thing was getting the press out to the shows. This is extremely difficult in England because the music press wields the power to make or destroy taste and they don't like anything they don't discover themselves.
Richey

We're very cynical people. We saw bands do all the pubs where we lived, do 200 gigs a year, get really big local followings, and they're all under the illusion that somebody from Sony Music will be driving through the middle of South Wales and go, 'Hey what a good band, let's sign here'. And of course we knew they never would. We knew we had to move to London.
Richey (1992)

At university I did politics and Richey did political history. That's where we've nicked all our lyrics from, really. We discovered the Sex Pistols and the Rolling Stones at the same time as we discovered literature. They seemed the same thing to us – both really exciting.
Nicky (1991)

While we were at University, James was on the dole and Sean worked at the civil service. He funded us, basically – when we were travelling about in Transit vans and paying to play at the Rock Garden. James was learning guitar – he's more dedicated than any of us.
Richey (1991)

When we started, we did want to conquer the world, but that was just a young boy's dream. The myth of complete arrogance, of thinking that you are the greatest band in the world. Which you only get one time in your life, usually when you're young, before you realise what it takes.
Nicky (1996)

We felt that we would change things. We called ourselves the Blue Generation for a while because we felt we were destined for collective greatness.
James (1996)

The only positive thing we could do was to be nihilistic. It was a good avenue to take, initially, but it didn't get us very far, did it?
James (1996)

We were a band before we even picked up guitars. And we didn't even know how, but we knew Richey had to be a part of it.
Nicky (1994)

We set out to be truly despised and hated.
Richey (1993)

We realised that as individuals we were very limited as people, so we had to fabricate ourselves and took a very academic approach at being a band. We were quite clinical. We were like magpies, collecting information, keeping dossiers on journalists and learning how to manipulate them.
Nicky

In the beginning, when we formed, we wanted to sign to the biggest record label in the world, put out a debut album that would sell 20 million and then break up. Get massive and then just throw it all away. By the time we were giving interviews and saying that to the press, though, we didn't believe it. We knew we couldn't quite do that. But if we had aimed any lower in the beginning, I don't think anyone would've paid as much attention to us.
Richey (1992)

We went down to (the) Underworld (club) one night. It was unbelievable. There were like five bands and loads of journalists, all drinking at the same tables. We were naive, but we never thought there would be that really close level of friendship. With most of the cool bands, you know the same people are going to write about them all the time... We just get people who really detest us.
Richey (1992)

Boys In The Band

We're a pretty moody band. One of us is always brooding…
James (1994)

From the age of ten I was very much isolated as an individual, entirely self-sufficient. I live from day to day.
Sean (1996)

It's very working class to want to better yourself. Me and Richey especially were attracted to being clever to prove that we were better than the other… plebs.
Nicky (1996)

I never needed people to love me. I revel in being hated. I just do. Well, not so much any more, but if people dislike me it gives me strength, whereas perhaps for Richey it didn't. There hasn't been anyone like Richey for the last ten years, with those intellectual demons inside him.
Nicky (1996)

I never consider James or Sean as musicians. They're friends. We're not a band chucked together from the back pages of *Melody Maker*. First and foremost we're friends.
Nicky (1996)

If you'd have gone into our houses when we were 20, you would have found the same books, the same records, the same videos. We were all attracted to the glamour of suicides and alcohol and beauty. That *Rumblefish* thing of self-destruction. It's just Richey took it a lot further than us. Ian Curtis and Kurt Cobain were the two Richey icons. The Hendrixes and the rest were just decadent. But Kurt and Ian had meant to do it – took control. That was more fascinating to Richey.
Nicky (1996)

Let's face it, you don't need any clues for Richey. Ever since he carved '4 Real' on his arm, nothing would surprise you. Alcoholic, anorexic, drugs, self-mutilator… all your favourite things rolled into one.
Nicky (1996)

There's a difference in Nick and Richey's lyrics. Richey could be quite nasty and classically nihilistic in that there was rage but no answers. But Nick's anger is translated into optimism.
James (1996)

One of the biggest things we needed when we were young was excitement. Music was the most important things in our lives. We probably are the loneliest people… I think we're the loneliest people I've ever met. Music and videos were everything.
Richey (1991)

We can be pretty stupid. We've always done dumbfuck things – Richey's arm, for instance. We give people more enjoyment than any other band going. The very fact we were from Wales meant there was no point trying to be cool…
Nicky (1991)

We've always got a kick out of goading people into thinking we were complete tossers.
James (1994)

I felt Richey was the oldest and yet the youngest of us all. He'd only experience things by forcing himself into situations. He was quite immature in terms of what he'd experienced in life: never been in a relationship, things like that.
James (1994)

We always open our mouths before we think. But that's part of where we come from, part of having fuck all to do all day and saying things to each other simply to create arguments. It was a way of getting through the day.
Richey (1993)

Things get taken to stupid proportions every time we talk; we come out with Mark E Smithisms. We're so comfortable in each other's company – we're talking about 15 years of friendship – that the whole politically correct mentality, avoiding saying certain things when we meet someone new, really doesn't apply.
Richey (1993)

People have still got this stupid idea that I'm a loud, aggressive person. That by the things I've done I'd be hyperactive, talking all the time, running around going 'rrarrarrarr', smashing people in the face, kicking down doors. Which is not the case. I've never destroyed anything in my life, apart from a few guitars.
Richey (1994)

I am not stupid. I might come across as stupid. That's nothing to do with academic qualifications. I think there's a difference between intelligence and knowledge. There are plenty of people with letters after their names who only know figures and dates. It's possible to know a lot of facts but not know anything at all.
Richey (1994)

I think everybody's first love is themselves. Some more than others. Some can divide themselves and give something of themselves to another person, which I've never been able to do because I've never trusted another person enough.
Richey (1994)

There's always something to be angry about. I think we've all tried to deny it at some point or another, but being unhappy and dissatisfied is part of our make-up. I look at my video collection or book collection and I realise they're all about fucked-up loners.
Nicky (1994)

If I was in a pub and someone attacked me, and I knew I'd done nothing wrong, I would happily take a beating without doing anything, and feel really superior. I would never hit somebody back. If I'd done something wrong it's different. But if I was minding my own business, I could easily take a kicking. I'd think, 'I don't give a fuck 'cos you are scum. You're way down there and I'm above you 'cos I can take it'. It's a bit Biblical, 'turn the other cheek' and all that.
Richey (1994)

I find the idea of Kurt Cobain taking his own life frighteningly powerful. I've always been a sucker for that.
Nicky (1994)

Nicky and Sean are still true to the spirit of the Manics, whereas Richey and I are tending to lose the plot a bit.
James (1994)

I have a very child-like rage and a very child-like loneliness.
Richey (1994)

Nick has deliberately made his life simple. The way he conducts his life is almost monastic.
James (1996)

Nick doesn't feel he has to experience anything directly in order to write about it. It's what I call 'homestead lyricism'. It's about admitting that you still feel wonder at the very basic things in life. When I used to get pissed out of my mind every night, I lost that wonder. I began to realise that perhaps Nicky had it right after all.
James (1996)

There's a poem by Tennessee Williams called 'Lament For Moths', one of the first poems we ever read, which is about how the moths, the sensitive people, will always be stamped on and crushed by the mammoths – that really hit us, the sudden realisation that we were the moths of the world.
Nicky (1994)

Richey feels things so fucking intensely. He always had this vision of purity, of perfection, a kind of childlike vision, that became completely obliterated. A misprint on a lyric sheet, or whatever, would just upset him so much, and he got to a stage where he just couldn't stop himself from doing anything.
Nicky (1994)

Richey never had as many setbacks as a kid as me, he's more acutely intelligent than me, he's more beautiful than me – and yet he has more problems. Problems that I'd just snip off with the fucking scissors in two seconds flat really get to Richey.
James (1994)

When we're not working, we phone each other up at least once a day. We're just big yappers.
James (1994)

I am a melodramatic drama queen, I can't help that. Everything I've ever liked in literature has been along those lines. I guess I identify with victims.
Richey (1994)

The band have never called me Richey. They've always called me Android, or something like that.
Richey (1994)

Richey has always been in love with rose-tinted perfection. So he was always in danger of being let down.
James (1994)

I've always found it hard to express how I feel, even from when I was a little child. It's a very British emotion – they keep things bottled up inside them. Some more than others.
Richey (1994)

I do consider myself to be something of a pretentious wanker.
Nicky (1993)

The difference between me and Richey is he always wanted to be understood, and I prefer being misunderstood. I don't feel the need for people to love or respect me, whereas Richey did.
Nicky (1994)

Everybody's got a corner of their heart and mind you can't get into. Richey was always much more into books and films than rock'n'roll, and I think those artforms are much more idealised. I think they influenced the way he viewed his life, and the way he thought it would be. I think of that quote in *Rumblefish*, y'know? 'He's merely miscast to play; he was born on the wrong side of the river'. He has the ability to do anything but he can't find anything he wants to do.
James (1994)

Richey was half Ian Curtis, half Iggy Pop.
Nicky (1995)

Richey: 4 Real

At the edge of eternity is torture, in our mind's never-ending ambition to damage itself.
Nicky (1993)

What made Richey the way he was? There is no dramatic thing, that's the scariest thing of all. To be honest, I think that, if anything, it's because his childhood was so happy that when he reached the age of responsibility, he couldn't handle it. He genuinely loved being young, but when you leave school, that's when the real world hits you. That's the most traumatic thing, having to grow up and realising – as he would put it – that everything was shit. Richey used to say 'you're born unmarked', then he'd look at himself and go, 'now I'm scarred'. They do say that 27 is the optimum time for males to commit suicide or break down, usually because of a longing for a disappearing youth.
Nicky (1996)

Living in a tower block with hundreds of other students was a really bad experience. I think if I'd been able to have a flat of my own, my memory would've been very different because I've never been good with very many people. I've always surrounded myself with just a few.
Richey (1994)

When I'm driving my car and the traffic lights turn red I think it's because I'm in the car. I feel persecuted...
Richey

Richey just reached a point where something clicked. His self-abuse has just escalated so fucking badly – he's drinking, he's mutilating himself, he's on the verge of anorexia...there's a line in 'Yes'; 'hurt myself to let the pain out'.

Richey just found it so hard to say no to anybody, and that really was his way of letting out pain.
Nicky (1994)

When I cut myself I feel so much better. All the little things that might have been annoying me suddenly seem so trivial because I'm concentrating on the pain... I'm not a person who can scream and shout so this is my only outlet. It's all done very logically.
Richey (1994)

The only people who are disturbed by Richey cutting himself are those who don't know him. They don't understand... We do know him, we do understand.
Sean (1994)

When it came for me to do my finals, I suddenly realised that I can't go in to do my finals pissed. So the way for me to gain control was cutting myself a little bit. Only with a compass – you know, vague little cuts – and not eating very much. That way I found I was really good during the day. I slept, I felt good about myself, I could do all my exams. I got a 2:1 so I wasn't a 100 per cent success, but I got through it. I did it.
Richey (1994)

You just get to a point where if you don't do it to yourself, you get a feeling that something really terrible is going to happen, and when that moment comes, it's the logical thing to do. It doesn't hurt. You're not screaming and shouting. A couple of days later you feel like a sad fuck, but that's part of the healing process: after that you feel really good. People that harm themselves, be it through anorexia or razors, know what they're doing.
Richey (1994)

The Infamous 4 Real incident

The first time I ever saw Richey cutting himself was at university, revising for his finals. And he just got a compass and went like that (draws invisible blade across arm). But I knew a lot of people at university who did that, so when he did '4 Real', obviously I was really shocked.
Nicky (1994)

I was really fucked off with (journalist) Steve Lamacq. I didn't know what I could possibly say to make him understand. How easy and cheap is it for me to just hit him? I would never want to do that. I would rather cut myself, because I feel I can justify that. Whereas I can't justify hitting him.
Richey (1994)

Self-mutilation in pop – you can trace it through from Iggy Pop to Julian Cope, but they just wanted to be seen as mad fucks. Richey is the least violent person I've met in my life and what he did just showed that as soon as a person is prepared to turn violence on themselves as a statement, people become totally shocked.
James (1992)

I tried talking to Steve (Lamacq) for an hour to explain ourselves. He saw us as four hero-worshipping kids trying to replicate our favourite bands. There was no way I could change his mind. I didn't abuse him or insult him, I just cut myself. To show that we are no gimmick, that we are pissed off, that we are for real.
Richey (1991)

The journalist was trying to say we were manufactured and just hero-worshipping past bands. We play rock'n'roll and we live rock'n'roll. Rock'n'roll is our lives.
Richey (1991)

We're completely happy that people despise us – but when you get a writer who should be in fanzines saying that he doesn't believe we meant it and that we're just a manager's invention, then I got so pissed off that I had to do it. That guy couldn't conceive that people can be so frustrated and pissed off that they're prepared to hurt themselves.
Richey (1991)

It was the only way to get through to a 24-year-old who thinks like a 45-year-old.
Richey (1991)

It shook us all up. We stood in disbelief, I think that was the beginning. Richey had always been very straight and normal through school and university. He was no-one you'd point a finger at and say 'he's strange'.
Sean (1996)

People should realise what the level of violence is like in most people's lives. It's sad that working-class resentment is always turned on itself. Nobody seems to realise that.
Richey (1992)

Breakdown

The reality of Richey's life is blurred by the way he disappeared. He might've known what was going on deep down, but what he gave out… you'd just wonder why small things would bother him immensely. When we were rehearsing he'd phone me 50 times to check the time.
Nicky (1996)

I don't think (Richey's breakdown) was a natural extension of being in a group. It might have accelerated it, that's all. In some ways, Richey's a very Richard Briers person, very cardigan, pipe and slippers. But I think if he'd gone on to become a lecturer – which he might well have done – the same thing could have very easily happened, perhaps in a more private way.
James (1994)

I'm weak, all my life I've felt weak compared to other people, if they want to crush me they can. But I know I can do things that other people can't.
Richey

In Portugal Richey and I were in the hotel watching dreadful European TV and we weren't on until four in the morning and I have never felt so bleak in my life. Richey was having a few crying sessions. He burst into tears after the gig and then, three months later, he had his first breakdown when he chopped himself up.
Nicky (1996)

I wasn't coping very well and I thought my body was probably stronger than it actually was. My mind was quite strong. I pushed my body further than it was meant to go. And then I went to hospital in Cardiff. That wasn't much good. The band came down to see me and it was pretty obvious that there wasn't much point in me staying there.
Richey (1994)

It was obvious he had to go to hospital. He realised it, we realised it, his parents realised it. He's just really ill in a lot of ways at the moment. Something's gone a bit awry, and I think he feels deep down it would have come to this whether he'd been a teacher or a bank clerk. I personally think being in a band has accelerated it.
Nicky (1994)

The way we see it is that he'll be back as soon as possible and if it comes to the point where he's not coming back, we won't continue.
Nicky (1994, on Richey's hospitalisation following a breakdown)

It's very romantic to think 'I'm a tortured writer', but mental institutions are not full of people in bands. They're full of people with so-called normal jobs. Or were full. 68,000 beds have been closed down in the last couple of years, which I wouldn't have been aware of unless I was actually in one.
Richey (1994)

The Priory (the private clinic where Richey was taken after his first breakdown) ripped out the man and left a shell. These people say they've got a cure, but that cure is to totally change your personality. You could see him struggling with this, wondering if this was the only way.
Nicky (1996)

I think it would make me angry if Richey's songwriting just became therapy.
James (1994)

We have to watch how we govern ourselves now. Without being corny, Richey and I were, if not quite birding and boozing buddies, something like that. We'd go out or stay up after the gigs. We can't do that now. I wouldn't want it for him. As far as his treatment is concerned, it's just not on the agenda. We don't want to be unfeeling dickheads.
James (1994)

A lot of groups would have got in another guitarist, but that wouldn't have been right for us. We were all quite numb to any sort of discussion about the group's future because we were all too concerned about Richey. We never entertained any discussion about the group until he brought it up himself.
James (1994, on playing five gigs while Richey was recovering from his breakdown)

Anorexia

It's a well known fact that anorexics try to cover up their condition with baggy clothes all the time. On the first day of the British tour, Richey walks in and he's wearing the tightest pair of girls' leggings that I've ever seen in my life. He still wanted the rest of the world to know he was completely fucked up.
Nicky (1996)

The best thing is knowing that no one can do a fucking thing about it. People can't actually hold you down and force food into your mouth. And someone can't be near you 24 hours a day to stop you doing something to your body. And ultimately they've got no right to, because it is your body.
Richey (1994)

We had so much poetry off anorexics and a lot of it was so shit even Richey was getting fed up – not another pile of this again. I said, 'look I'm gonna have to write a song taking the piss out of their poetry', and he was laughing. Even though he was one – or at least half anorexic – he could still see what I meant. He'd go, 'Oh no, not another fucking poem about eating an apple in the morning'.
Nicky (1996)

The worst thing I did was to keep trying to be normal, which is how I ended up in hospital. Now I wake up in the morning and I know what I want to do – I want to write, it makes me feel better in myself… I value writing songs, I do regard myself as a good poet. I work hard. Songwriting is an art and I really try my best at it.

The band is getting better and better, the lyrics are too. I've found better ways to express myself… I don't think I've changed what I say but maybe I'm saying it in a different way.
Richey (1995)

Richey was too vain to admire people like himself. He got so sick of anorexics coming up and offering him peaches.
Nicky (1996)

We had to put (Richey) to bed one night 'cos he just burst out crying in the car. And then he phoned me up at about half-three in the morning and – you know those terrible commercial presentations you get? Some American twat showing you how to flatten your stomach or summat – he phoned me up, and we were watching that together, and it seemed so bleak and nondescript. We didn't have a row or anything, but he kept yapping and I was really tired. The next morning, he comes up to me and he says, 'Here you are, Wire.' And he gave me a fucking Mars bar, as a little present.
Nicky

Early evening I walk around Soho on my own as I have so few friends. It starts to rain. And even cheap dreams don't stop the rain.
Richey (1992)

There's a trigger in Richey that he can't control. He doesn't have a second skin. He has a mental illness… You can do all you can, but you can't put someone in a strait-jacket. It's a cliché, but you can only be there for the fall.
James (1994)

I'd love to love someone seriously, but considering what I'd expect and what would be expected of me it seems quite difficult. I feel nobody would want to live with me. To love somebody involves being trapped by jealousy. It's really hard. I never wanted to love somebody insincerely – and I don't mean sexually, but intellectually and mentally too... Seriously, if I was in love with a woman, she'd have to be more attractive than Bette Davis, more than anyone else. I'd peel every picture off my walls.
Richey (1995)

Tony Hancock's suicide note ('things just went wrong too many times') is one of the most beautiful things I've ever read.
Richey (1992)

The last thing I wanted to do was end up a fucking junkie alcoholic mess like Shane McGowan [sic]. The thing about self-harm is that you are aware of what you're doing. That's how you justify it... It's the arbitrary factors that determine your life.
Richey (1994)

In terms of the 'S' word, that does not enter my mind. And it never has done. In terms of An Attempt. Because I am stronger than that. I might be a weak person, but I can take pain.
Richey (1994)

On the Suede tour in 1994, I was aware that, for the first time ever in my life, I was starting to grow away from Richey. He came out of the Priory, full of this 12-point recovery programme and all that shit, and he just wasn't the same person any more as far as I was concerned.
Nicky (1995)

If I can't sleep I tend to have destructive ideas and I have to do something to root them out. I couldn't sleep and all I could think of was shaving my head, so I did. I can sleep now. I was almost in love with my hairstyle. But in the end I just felt like abandoning things like that.
Richey (1995)

Walking On The Edge

Drugs...

Drugs are the biggest get-out clause in the world. Dope enhances your creativity? Bollocks! It destroys your brain cells. When we came to London it was 'hey, chill out, spliff up man'. But our calling-card was 'Anxiety is freedom'.
Nicky (1996)

I think we're going to have drug problems and end up living in a squat in south London.
Richey (1992)

On our first European tour I remember us going to Frankfurt and seeing the needles at the station and being so shocked. We had never had anything to do with that.
Nicky (1996)

I could never see the argument that *Trainspotting* glamorised heroin, 'cos I think it's incredibly seedy, but the very fact that handsome actors are making loads of money doing a brilliant film is obviously glamorous. Drugs, for me, I just find them incredibly boring and I find the people that take them incredibly boring.
Nicky (1996)

I must admit, in all my years in the industry, cocaine seems back with a vengeance. It hardly breeds reasoned behaviour, but it sometimes breeds good records...
Nicky (1996)

... and drink

On the Suede tour James was pissed all the time and was lying in bed until five every day. I had my moments.
Sean (1996)

I started drinking in my first term at university. It was something that I'd never allowed myself to do, but it was just a question of getting to sleep. It was so noisy, and I needed to get to sleep at a certain time and wake at a certain time. Drinking gave me that opportunity.
Richey (1994)

It's true that I drink at least half a bottle of vodka a day, but it's only on the same level as most people. Say if we were back home, working: everybody I know would

come home from work, go down to the pub, drink five or six pints, forget about everything and go to bed. I don't think it's a big thing...
Richey (1993)

At least a third of my body must have been made of alcohol during the run-up to the release of 'A Design For Life'. I just didn't feel confident. You'd go home to see your mum and dad and she'd go, 'James, I never thought you'd have a weight problem! Look at your dad'. And my dad's there, 55 years old, smokes 40 a day, drinks and he's completely fit and hard. My auntie comes in and goes, 'Oooh, you fat little blob'.
James (1996)

I'm trying not to drink. You can't play the kind of shows we do if you're permanently hungover.
Sean (1996)

I'm the sort of person who wakes up in the morning and needs to pour a bottle down my throat… I'm paranoid about not being able to sleep and if by about eight o'clock at night I haven't had a drink, I get massive panic attacks and I'll be awake all night, and that's my biggest nightmare. I know that until one in the afternoon I'm going to be shaky and have cold sweats. By six o'clock I feel good, but by eight it starts coming round again, the thought of not sleeping. And that's when I start drinking.
Richey (1994)

The one constant in Richey's life which he enjoyed was drinking. The fact that it put him to sleep. He'd drink on his own – not a social thing.
Nicky (1996)

My need is functional. By about midday I need a drink to stabilise me, but I've got to drive the group to rehearsal, so I can't have that drink. But on tour, I drink all day, just so I don't have to think about going onstage.
Richey (1994)

Typical rock bands drink Jack Daniels and get fucked-up because they have this romantic, glamourous Jack Kerouac vision of the world. When I sit in my bedroom with a book and a bottle of vodka, I do it because I'm sad, not 'cos I think it's cool. I do it because I want to forget what I'm thinking about.
Richey (1992)

I used to be really outgoing, but I'm more withdrawn now than I ever was. I can almost honestly say that I've seen Richey and James become confirmed alcoholics over the last 18 months. During that period there hasn't been a single day where Richey hasn't had at least half a bottle of vodka. Neither him or James can go to sleep at night without drinking that much. It's depressing. If they went out boasting about it, it would be worse.
Nicky (1993)

At university, I never spent my money on beer like all the union crowd. I just used to go into town and play on the fruit machines. I got to be a bit of an expert at it. In fact I was completely addicted, and I ended up £3,000 in debt because of it. I've never drank or taken a single drug in my life, so I guess fruit machines took their place.
Nicky (1994)

Sex

I was about 12, playing football and a bloke called Brian Summers said, 'I've found some great stuff under my brother's bed'. It was quite hardcore porn. We all had a look at it, about five of us, in silence for ten minutes, then I had to run out the house quite quickly. I was ill. I was sick.
Richey (1994)

I was 12 and I used to mess around with a mate down the street in his garage, and his father kept loads of porn magazines in there. I was just really turned on by it. It awakens all your interest. It was my rites of passage sexually, definitely.
James (1994)

I've seen loads of porn films. When I was 16 we used to go to a friend's house every dinner time and we watched this same porn film every lunchtime solidly for a month. You got bored after a while, mostly because there was no way you could sneak upstairs to the toilet and just stay there for ten minutes because everyone would kill themselves laughing when you came back.
James (1994)

If you're on tour you might stop off at a service station and buy a porn magazine. It's usually chucked away before you even get back on the bus. It's banal entertainment. They're all identical. Films too. You've seen one porn film, there's no point watching another. The only interest is when somebody gets something like *Animal Farm*, chickens and ducks. Yeah, I've seen it. After five minutes it's boring because it's just the same thing with a different animal.
Richey (1994)

All bands go to sex shops. When you tour Germany and Holland, that's what you do. I've been in one in Britain and it was so limp-wristed that I walked straight out. I'm too used to the hard stuff.
James (1994)

I think that sex between two people is quite crushingly dull. All the magazines here… I really can't find anything sexy in them. Men with non-erect dicks or man on top of woman, woman on top of man – it just bores the fuck out of me. Essentially porn is for 13-year-old kids.
Richey (1994)

The thrill of pornography is coming, and I think that wastes away into wanting something better. It makes me more romantic. It's a classic male response: you get pornography, you get your kicks out of it, then suddenly you think, 'Oh, I'm not really into that, because I want a relationship'. Does that make be a better person or a worse person? I don't know.
James (1994)

We got asked by *For Women* if we would appear naked, but I have no desire to expose my genitalia. Too small.
Richey (1994)

That Wonderbra advert might be funny, but it's still designed to titillate men. We'd be kidding ourselves if we didn't say that's a picture of a woman being subservient to a little sexual token, a bra.

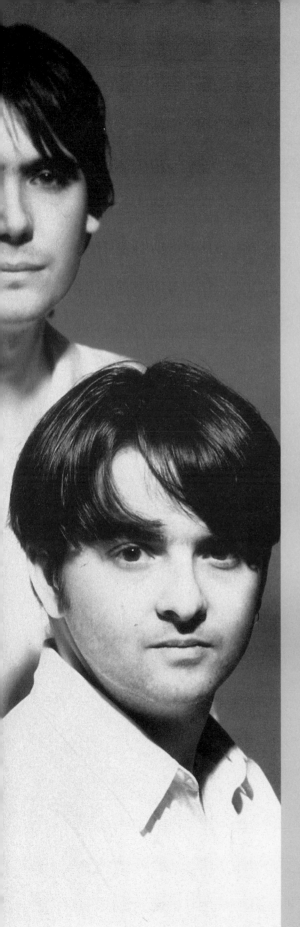

Advertising men use feminine images as subservient to everything. And *Penthouse* and *Playboy* try to diffuse pornographic images by putting in features about cars, or lifestyles of the rich and famous. That's just backing up the advertising industry. It's fusing pornography and product. It's very tactful. It pisses me off.
James (1994)

I find it very sad that a girl in a swimming costume is all that's required to turn some men on.
Sean (1994)

I don't regard paying for sex as being that different to sleeping with a groupie. It's all done on the same functional level.
Richey (1994)

We like to threaten people sexually. Especially males.
Nicky (1993)

We all love to play the fruit machines but Sean owed thousands of pounds. The problem got so bad our record company had to pay off all our debts for us, and they banned us from gambling ever again.
Richey (1992)

Porn has helped me through fallow periods. Everyone goes through a dodgy period when they can't pull anything. Porn just gives you a quick relief. It just sends you to sleep really… men just want to see women with their legs open.
James (1994)

Sex is just an iota removed from a wank.
Richey (1991)

I think people are becoming more machine like and that's the imagery I like. Also sex and death are closely linked. Sado-masochistic imagery, bleeding… I find it attractive. I find it… sexual.
Richey (1994)

I've had herpes since I was 15.
Nicky (1991)

Songwriting And Recording

We aren't wallowing in any musical nostalgia like the music papers' Clash/Dylan freaks. We might sound like the last 30 years of rock'n'roll, but our lyrics address the same issues as Public Enemy.
Richey (1991)

We must write our thoughts without any regard for structure or tone. It's up to James to fit it in. Sometimes he has a really impossible line, or something he doesn't want to sing, so he cuts it. We usually give him a page of words and let him choose. We've never cared about our lyrics being cut up. Some of our favourite authors, like Burroughs, did that anyway. Kerouac never used full stops or commas.
Richey (1991)

You can never get the producer you want (for *Generation Terrorists*). We wanted Public Enemy, but that was impossible to produce the whole album. I'm glad they didn't do it, actually. I wouldn't want them working with a poxy band like us.
Nicky (1991)

We can only really make basic, straightforward white rock music, 'cos we're not patronising people. We don't pretend we understand the street, or pretend to understand New York City. You know, we live in a crap little town in Britain.
Richey (1991)

I currently spend eight or ten hours a day playing *Sonic The Hedgehog* on my Megadrive. That's all I've done while the others have been making the LP (*Generation Terrorists*). It took me a couple of weeks, to get to the end and kill Doctor Robotnik. Then, every day, I couldn't live with myself unless I tried to finish Sonic in a shorter time. I should be interested in learning to play my guitar, but Sonic The Hedgehog rules my life. I find that very sad. It's the same with Nick, having to go up and play on a fruit machine every day.
Richey (1991)

We'll never write a love song. We'll be dead before we have to do that.
Richey (1990)

I have to totally understand everything I'm singing, it's not just a throwaway thing. I think of myself as a redeemable Roger Daltrey.
James (1994)

When we write lyrics, sometimes we'll come up with something we think is really good and works really well with James' melody. And I hate having the thought in the back of my head that we can't possibly print this in a lyric sheet, because people will misunderstand it.
Richey (1994)

I've been getting better as a guitarist and did actually play some guitar on this record (*Gold Against The Soul*). But I don't know if that was just to amuse the other members.
Richey (1993)

We recorded *Gold Against The Soul* in a fucking £2,000 a day studio. Snooker tables, swimming pools – and I thought, 'Shit, I'm turning into Primal Scream', you know, just hanging out, spending money. Something had to change, so we wrote, rehearsed and recorded this album (*The Holy Bible*) in some shithole studio in the red light district of Cardiff. Not going out, just working and working, listening to Joy Division records, working, working some more.
Nicky (1994)

Richey's written about 70 per cent of this album (*The Holy Bible*). He just kept handing us complete lyrics that were absolutely perfect, absolutely beautiful and very personal. He's not here to speak for himself, but I think he's explained himself pretty fucking perfectly in those songs.
Nicky (1994)

'Of Walking Abortions' (The Holy Bible) was one of the most extreme examples of Richey's lyrics – 'so wash your car in your X baseball shoes'. I just didn't know what the fuck he was on about. All the weight of reference to Eastern Europe or Nazi culture and figureheads. 'Revol'? I didn't have a clue what that was about. Even Richey said afterwards that he didn't know what it was about. It's lover spelt backwards, or so he kind of tried to explain it. A decline in relationships… I don't know.
Nicky (1997)

The Holy Bible was created through an almost academic discipline. We sat down and gave ourselves headings and structures, so each song's like an essay.
James (1994)

I don't see The Holy Bible as a record, I see it as a state of mind. One we were all in. When we recorded it Richey wasn't suicidal or anything. He'd just bought a flat, he was still drinking and he'd come in about 12 o'clock, collapse and have a snooze and say 'Leave me alone, I've had a big drink' in a nice Welsh voice. Then he'd get up and do a bit of typing and we'd record for a bit, then go round Cardiff and have a shop.
Nicky (1996)

I was worried that, because Richey was undergoing treatment, he'd turn into Peter Gabriel, lyrically. He's living on a different proverb a day at the moment and I didn't want our songs to turn into psychobabble. But he's kept his own voice, which is admirable. It hasn't weakened us, but I'm not prepared to say it's made us stronger.
James (1994)

When I was young I used to keep myself to myself. I don't feel I have the right to intrude on anyone else, and I don't think anyone should necessarily want to listen to me. I think my lyrics are valid. I guess it's egotistical to publish your lyrics, but we always publish them because I want people to read them.
Richey (1994)

We thought 'Motorcycle Emptiness' was universal, and I still think it's fantastic. But 'life lies a slow suicide' and 'culture sucks down words' – it doesn't translate literally. A song like 'Yes' (The Holy Bible), which was a brilliant song, there were so many words there, and so many difficult words, that it was impossible for James to sing it. And if James can't sing it, there's no way a crowd can sing it, and there's no way you can digest it from the radio.
Nicky (1997)

I'm in a privileged position of interpretation. Sean and I never use bits of music we have lying around. We start afresh when we hear the lyrics. I have rules: I don't have to accept, only understand.
James (1994)

This time we seemed to be capable of saying everything we wanted to say. We weren't shoehorning the lyrics in this time, the lyrics suggested the melodies, these beautiful, beautiful melodies. James is so happy with this record, (The Holy Bible) and he's not a man who's easily pleased.
Nicky (1994)

I don't think we've ever made happy records. Maybe we've had uplifting moments, but I don't think lyrically we've ever been particularly joyous.
Richey (1994)

Sleep is constantly throughout every lyric I've ever written. It's a big thing because I'm scared to go to sleep. 'Cos the things I get in my head I don't like. That's the reason I started drinking – to knock me out.
Richey (1994)

Richey would always find something new to write about. Always. Whether it was a disease, or an article he read… he would always find some obscure reference which two people in the world knew about.
Nicky (1997)

I would like to be able to write 'I'm feeling supersonic, give me gin and tonic', but I just can't. I think that's a brilliant lyric, but I haven't felt supersonic since I was about ten years old.
Richey (1994)

We've always had a song about disease on every one of our albums. It's not a very good tradition to follow, really.
Nicky (1996)

People want well-played, good, sensibly-dressed songs, so I've convinced myself it's a kind of tactic to get in a position where perhaps the bigger we get it might be easier to subvert. Maybe then we'll dress up again and I'll strip again like I did in Thailand. If I've still got the guts to do it.
Nicky (1996)

I was like the McCartney to Richey's Lennon. But even Richey's lyrics on this album (Everything Must Go) are quite easy to understand. 'Black Flowers' is about something; 'Kevin Carter' is about something. With The Holy Bible and songs like 'Revol', people didn't have a clue what it was about. Richey was so intelligent that he ended up trying to condense so much that it was unintelligible.
Nicky (1997)

'A Design For Life' is one of the best songs we've ever written. 'Motorcycle Emptiness' is one of the best songs of the decade, but there was no way it could be a hit in 1992. British culture was so divided: the Levellers, the arse end of Madchester, shoegazing, acid house. But I think we knew straight away with 'Design'. James phoned me

after he'd written it and said it was something special. Ennio Morricone, a bit of Tamla, a bit of Spector. Our only reservation was it might be too epic.
Nicky (1996)

Having (producer) Mike Hedges around (for Everything Must Go) helped. Boring to say though it is, we can play now. It's so much easier to record now that I can keep up with James a bit.
Nicky (1996)

All our records are just collages of ideas, a reflection of our bedrooms. Our first album was an attempt to find answers from Public Enemy, Guns N' Roses, McCarthy and the Clash. I'm under no illusion that Everything Must Go is original either. Pick a song and I'll tell you exactly which records it comes from. I don't think we're original, but I think we're unique.
James (1996)

James loves all that Motown stuff, it's all he fucking plays on the bus. It's his sexmusic. You can hear it on Everything Must Go, even if it's clouded by a few rockisms.
Nicky (1996)

We're not saying that we've got to forget our past. Things like that will always be with you. But obviously, it is a new start in some ways. We did feel a bit free doing the album (Everything Must Go) – it is such a reaction against The Holy Bible, musically.
Nicky (1996)

Mike Hedges uses old gear but we didn't go there (Normandy, France) for a full-on rustic valve experience. He's one of the last old-school fellas who really knows what he's doing with a band.
James (1996)

Our first three albums were a build up to this one (Everything Must Go). They're all flawed mind, occasionally naive records, but they were important. The Holy Bible was very dark, something we knew from

the moment we started working on it that wasn't going to be played at parties. But without Richey, we've become more optimistic on record, more positive. Having said that, I think some of the drama has gone now he's not around.
Sean (1996)

Everything Must Go is a more uplifting album than the ones we've done before. And it's what we wanted to do. We didn't want to make another mano-depressive album. We couldn't cope with going through the same misery again. But it's

still a pretty dark album. In the position we were in, it was pretty easy to write, a lot of emotions surfaced and we only needed to catch that.
Nicky (1996)

James has a lot of ideas and, musically, I think the next record will probably be a bit more adventurous, a fusion of the polar opposites of *The Holy Bible* and *Everything Must Go*. But to be honest, I'm finding it really hard to write any lyrics. I'm really struggling, I've got writer's block.
Nicky (1997)

Street Level

Signing to a major record company is the price of an education. We don't care what they do to us. The credibility of indie labels is shit.
Nicky (1991)

The whole indie mentality that grew up from punk onwards just seemed so bullshit to us, because the most subversive, really important group in the world were Public Enemy, and they were on Columbia (CBS/Sony, the Manics' label). The level of corruption on an indie label is just on a smaller scale.
Richey (1992)

Music industry is the easiest thing. The press, easy. Press agents, easy. All of them, easy. There's all these little boys going round being scared by it. It's all gone wrong. The independent mentality of the press sums it up. They're all tossers.
Richey (1991)

Everyone we talk to, we say 'We're not signing unless it's a contract for just one double album, one debut double'. Then we'll make enough money from that to last forever.
Nicky (1991)

'Everything Must Go' was a proper hit because blokes in my mum's betting shop were whistling it.
James (1996)

To be universal, you've got to stain the consciousness of the people. You've got to dig out a truth that everybody knows, but they don't want to hear, then tell it in a manner that's so articulate and so aesthetically indignant, so beautiful, that they've got to accept it back in their lives again.
James (1996)

We've had quite a few letters saying we're a band parents like, because we're quite moral and intelligent. I think they've gained that impression from the new album *(Everything Must Go)*. They might not be so keen if they heard us do 'Repeat'.
Nicky (1997)

We know it's a pointless existence being in a band. It's not a worthwhile job, like being a doctor or a nurse. There are people who work for nothing saving badgers or otters.
Richey (1991)

It's the ideal prototype. Do one brilliant album then disappear, gain everything then give it away, create this franchise then scrap it.
James (1991)

Whatever happens to us, at least we'll know that we always tried to be a brilliant band. We've set ourselves up to be compared with the greatest rock bands ever. We've always set out to be something worthwhile, that meant something real and valuable; to make records about ideas and attitudes that are important and real, and that no one else is doing. To be the band we never had when we were growing up.
Richey (1991)

If we'd fulfilled the promise of the ten million albums then I'd be running for the President of America by now. It wouldn't have changed us... except maybe to accelerate our decline.
Nicky (1996)

Even Richey's self-mutilation was very private. His fuck-ups were not on public display. There was a working-class disgust – cover it up and get on with it. I have a concept of a working-class rage which is in some people. It's in us. It's in Liam Gallagher, Linford Christie, Nigel Benn and Paul Gascoigne. The desire to prove yourself.
Nicky (1996)

We got signed to Sony for a lot of money, but none of us bought anything, except portable CD players and stuff. Then, two months later, another one came out that was thinner and I bought that one. It was no value to my life, it just means I have a smaller CD player.
Richey (1991)

Whatever we've achieved, we never see it as any kind of achievement.
Nicky (1994)

My mind is not cluttered with the day-to-day necessities of staying alive. I'm not worried about 'if I don't pay this bill the gas is gonna get cut off'. Because I just chuck some money to somebody and it gets paid.
Richey (1994)

I had some fun a couple of days ago. That's my lot for a while.
Sean (1994)

When the gigs are getting bigger and people love you more and there's all this euphoria, it's harder to get quite so angry.
Nicky (1997)

The band was never about self-hate, it was about injustice in society and with *The Holy Bible* it became too inward-looking for my liking… It was never the intention to carry on in that vein, but now we're destined to be frozen in time as this myth. The only way we could ever break out of that now is to completely shed all our old fans, which I don't want to do.
Nicky (1996)

We were never a fanclub kind of band. We were hardly known for, you know, 'we love our fans'. We were never the kind of band who'd hang around signing autographs or whatever, but I think ultimately we gave them something a bit more special than that. We gave them a part of our lives.
Nicky (1996)

As long as we're the absolute antithesis of another main voice in pop music, then that's justification. A lot of groups who're massive now, like Blur or, especially, Pulp, they've got big by creating a certain empathy with their audience. And I don't think we're doing that now.
James (1996)

If you start off working at a certain level of intensity, you'll always be judged by that. It's easy, especially in a world as impatient and unforgiving as pop, to be rendered irrelevant by.your past actions.
James (1996)

I'll only be happy if we keep changing and moving forward, which is perhaps why the second album upset me a bit. I'm very protective about our history, and I wouldn't want to sully it.
James (1996)

The fact that 95 per cent of *New Musical Express* readers say they feel an affinity with Richey, or feel the need to support him, pre-empts the fact that the last five per cent think he's a cunt. They actually think he's playing up to the people who feel an affinity for him, for what he went through. They feel it's just another little angle, that's all.
James (1994)

I'm just as happy having people loathe me as I am to have them love me. Music's got safe and ordinary; it'd be good if a few more bands tried to get those sort of opinions forced on them.
Richey (1993)

We don't want to reach the music papers, we just want to reach *The Sun*, *The Star*, *The Mirror*. That's what most people read. We'd rather be sensationalised than just be another *NME* band and get critical respect. Critical respect is the easiest thing in the world because journalists are so crap.
Nicky (1990)

We know they (Sony) completely own us, they can do anything they want with us. They can drop us… In fact they said, 'If you want, you can come in and smash the place up, it would be good press'. It wouldn't be good press – we'd end up paying for it.
Richey (1991)

All Richey does is go to London, drives around in the Sony limousine, goes to Soho strip joints, spends £300 on the band's American Express card, comes back covered in love bites and asks how the track's going. I think that's the thing that's given me the most pride in this band.
Nicky (1992)

We wanted to sign to the biggest record label in the world, put out a debut album that would sell 20 million and then break up. Get massive and then just throw it all away.
Richey (1993)

Whether we sell millions and millions of albums, or we fail abjectly, we'll still have said everything we have to say in one double album. We don't want to look beyond that, because we'd just be treating it as a career. If you throw it away when you're the biggest band in the world, then you're bound to get respect.
Nicky (1991)

We signed to Sony for a quarter of a million in advance with £400,000 to make the album.
Nicky (1991)

I think a lot of our fans are motivated by the fact that other people hate them because they like us.
Nicky (1991)

A lot of girls of 14, 15 love the band. I think they see us raging on their side. I hate men. Males don't seem to have any self-control any more; something catches their eye and they don't see why they shouldn't have it.
Nicky (1992)

Preaching Live

It's really hard for us to take other bands out on tour. There's just no-one we can get on with or like, really. We're such an insular band, and musically we just seem poles apart from anybody. Lyrically also. We've just got nothing in common with anyone. I think that's because people are scared to do what we're doing.
Nicky (1993)

I don't look forward to touring… I don't like it. I don't like travelling and I can't sleep at hotels. I hate flying, actually. I don't know why I do it, really.
Nicky (1996)

(Supporting Oasis) is a good experience. You can't help but be proud when you hear the Oasis crowd sounding like they're at a schoolboy international, except there's lots of girls there too. It's humbling all the same. It puts you in your place.
James (1996)

We used to walk on to a reading of *Howl* by Allen Ginsberg. Not many bands did that in 1990. Not many bands do it now. I'm glad we did those things. They made us different. Most people thought we were pretentious wankers, which undoubtedly we were.
Nicky (1996)

Any other group in the world would get the audience to do this (claps hands above head) during the quiet bit of 'Roses In The Hospital' but we physically can't do it. We can't bond with the audience.
James (1994)

Doing the Suede tour in Europe was probably the worst time of my life. Richey wasn't well and I felt ill. I had all these pains. I flew home and went to a Harley Street doctor who said 'You want to watch the fruit out there; they don't wash it, these foreigners'. Fucking Harley Street doctor!
Nicky (1996)

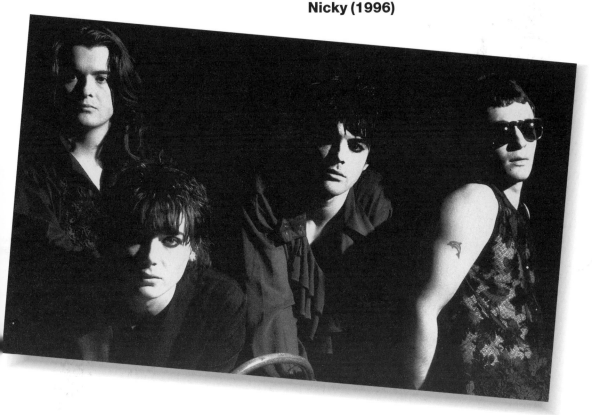

When we released *Generation Terrorists* we didn't play 'Motorcycle Emptiness' (live) for six months, because Richey and I couldn't play it.
Nicky (1996)

I feel very sad. This is the first time we've done concerts for a while. The last time we were really excited, talking among ourselves all the time. Now we sit on the four back seats of the tour bus, nobody really talking, playing computer games, listening to our CD players.
Richey (1991)

The first gig at the Whisky A-Go-Go in LA was just abusive; non musical. Totally and utterly nonsensical to the Americans. Made us realise that to break America is just about the hardest thing to do, especially if you're a British band.
Nicky (1996)

It's quite glamorous being associated with such a mad tour (Oasis). People not turning up, people disappearing. It's good that it wasn't us for a change. We were dead normal, professional. Didn't say a word.
Nicky (1996)

We're caught in between markets. We're not pop, we're not metal – our rockisms have always been a bit too synthetic for American tastes – and we're not alternative enough.
Nicky (1996)

I still think touring's one of the worst things you can do. I'd much rather be at home now watching the Welsh rugby match tonight. I'm just not into the experience, really. TV is such an integral part of my life and when you go abroad there's nothing you can watch.
Nicky (1996)

I used to have that *Barfly* mentality. It made it worthwhile travelling all this way to have almost Zen-like insights by meeting a stranger at a bar and having a good old yap. But even I've gone off that romanticism.
James (1996)

I feel much more comfortable in Europe now. There's just a general air that people have a bit of intelligence and a bit of humour. Even Germans have some sense of humour compared to (Americans). So I do feel really comfortable in Europe. Not happy, but comfortable.
Nicky (1996)

For me, being in a band is about expression. It used to be through image and nastiness, but now it's just through the lyrics. I love listening to music but I just get bored. I get utterly bored sometimes being in a band. I don't know how people can actually enjoy being on-stage in terms of playing. I still say the best five minutes ever of us being in a band was the last gig with Richey at the Astoria when we smashed everything up. That's the most enjoyment I've ever had onstage. It says something about myself.
Nicky (1996)

I'm enjoying Bangkok. I've never been on an 18-30s holiday before… I just feel like a complete lad. I don't feel any need to be accepted by women whatsoever, which is the way I've always felt, so it's reassuring to be me for once.
James (1994)

Tonight the gig was total shit. It's not that I need to bond with an audience at all, but I want it to be a good show, a spectacle. If things go wrong then it's all a waste of time and you might as well be a bloody travelling salesman. But I suppose it feels good to be wanted. That wasn't always the case.
James (1996)

When you go abroad there's so much pressure for you to experience things, to go out for these fancy meals every night, and I find it really boring. I don't mind going to an art gallery, or looking at the odd bit of architecture, but… I don't think   food is culture.
Nicky (1997)

The thrill of it isn't stardom. It's not all down to ego, 'cos I lost a lot of ego a long time ago. the thrill is that we're

going to be playing to all these people on the tour. Just the fact that you think 'I could do something tonight that might change somebody's life.'
Nicky (1996)

I suggested that I wouldn't play on stage anymore, but would carry on writing words and doing the artwork and stuff. I convinced myself that was what I wanted. But it's not enough for me just to do the words. I think I'd be cheating on them, 'cos the touring part is the worst bit – the bit that no band really enjoys. It's the thing that makes it feel like a job because you know what you'll be doing in three months time at two o'clock in the afternoon.
Richey (1994)

Glastonbury just seemed like the worst gig we'd ever done, it was like cabaret for post-degree students.
James (1994)

In Thailand, definitely for Richey and me, something just snapped. It isn't that we weren't getting on. We went to Portugal and had a terrible time and then Richey's friend from university hung himself and, from then on that summer, it got worse.
Nicky (1994)

Playing live without Richey is the one thing that's incomprehensible. Recording's not a problem. We are incredibly arrogant, we still think we're the best group in the world, we still think that we write the best songs. But without the visual iconoclastic weight of Richey, as well as missing him, it's not right.
Nicky (1996)

The more touring you do, the less you remember you have to talk to each other – but I think we'll have the dignity to get out before we turn into wretches.
Nicky (1993)

Heroes And Influences

(Seeing 'Guns N' Roses) was the first time that we realised rock wasn't dead. We had the Stones, the Who, the Clash and we'd basically given up on hearing a new rock record that we'd really like. When we heard this *(Appetite For Destruction)* it was just so instant and exciting.

'Sweet Child O' Mine' is one of the most amazing love songs ever written and 'Welcome To The Jungle' is one of the most hateful, but people just dismiss him (Axl) as a redneck. He's one of the few people I'd actually like to meet and talk to.
Richey

Music had got so tame and watered down, and all of a sudden Public Enemy were probably the most extreme band that's ever appeared. There's nothing more articulate or intelligent in the entire world.
Nicky (1993)

Oasis have made me a fan again. They've completely revitalised British music. But yeah, we do like to think it could have been us. Perhaps we didn't have the guile. We were too nasty and confrontational. We waged war on the punters, the music press, everyone.
Nicky (1996)

Nick tried to get Jocky Wilson's autograph once and Jocky just went 'Fuck off'. Nick's quite proud of that. We all loved the darts on the telly and things like *Pebble Mill*. When that closed down we shed a tear.
Richey (1992)

(Miners' leader) Arthur Scargill came to see us in Liverpool. He came back and had a chat, which was a bit of a magic moment. I still find him inspiring because, despite all his faults, everything he said came true.
Nicky (1997)

Meeting Arthur Scargill was the most nervous I've been this year. I found it scary that here was someone who had a lot in common with my uncles, but had found a way to articulate it all. But he was the worst strategist in the world. I just looked at him and immediately had a million questions in my head. You could talk to him all night and it would be as frustrating as it would be inspirational.
James (1997)

Musically I do genuinely love Oasis. They're so natural, I think it's above criticism. But I now know we're too difficult for that. They have something that hits you like an elemental force. In many ways, Oasis are the band we wanted to be, but never could be.
Nicky (1997)

When we supported Oasis at Maine Road, it just put everything in perspective. It made me realise that we were becoming a big band, but we were nowhere near becoming a phenomenon, and we never would. Maine Road showed us our allotted position. I knew what we never would be after that gig. People have taken Oasis so completely to their hearts, independent of anything like a marketing push, anything at all, it just seemed uncontrollable. Totally inspiring.
James (1997)

For us Public Enemy are the ultimate rock'n'roll band at the moment because they've got style and rage, which is what it's all about. So many bands are just worthless. We adore people like Kylie because she doesn't pretend to be anything except someone who makes brilliant pop records.
Richey (1991)

Alice In Chains are one of our favourite bands at the moment. They're like the American version of Joy Division, but a lot louder
Nicky (1994)

(Joy Division singer Ian Curtis was) the only musician whose death I was saddened by. I love music, but I couldn't give a fuck if anybody dropped dead tomorrow, I wouldn't shed a tear.
Richey

One of my heroes is Jimmy McGovern. He wrote *Cracker* and some of the early *Brookside* episodes. I've always really liked him, but I'd never seen him before last Sunday, when he was on the *South Bank Show*. He was absolutely fantastic. I loved all the *Crackers* he wrote, especially 'To Be Somebody' with Robert Carlyle as the Liverpool fan, which was one of the finest things I've ever seen.
Nicky (1996)

Everything I've liked has always failed in some way.
Richey (1994)

Although people might not think it, the Stone Roses did have a lasting influence on us when we started. They were people we defined ourselves against.
Nicky (1996)

Black people have got a far more genuine rage than a white man could ever have. White people feel repressed, but black people are completely oppressed – so you get a real militancy. Public Enemy combined that with being glamorous: the way they moved, the way they dressed – it was like Aretha Franklin on smack.
Richey (1993)

One lyricist I really admire is (Beautiful South singer) Paul Heaton, who's a real pop genius, but he still has a lot of depth in his lyrics, and his interviews are fantastic – when he goes on about being a Sheffield football hooligan: 'those people with the season tickets, they didn't give a fuck, it was the hooligans who kept Sheffield United going in the 1980s'. From a man who writes two-million-selling albums, I've got a lot of time for him.
Nicky (1997)

It's obvious to me that Oasis are the best band in the world. Liam is not very eloquent or anything, but you've just got to look at him and you know he's the business. He could have only come from where he came from.
Nicky (1996)

Image

I was never very interested in clothes back then (at university), and I never shopped at thrift shops. I was a bit of a nerdy casual. I was into golf so I even used to wear Pringle jumpers. We did used to get stuff from Oxfam when we started spray-painting shirts for the band, but that's different. It was only the rich kids that wanted to dress down like that.
Nicky (1994)

Individually we've always been pretty powerless, but together we make up for each others' inefficiencies. Nick's handsome and has always been the most popular with the girls; Richey never had any musical talent but he's so articulate and sensitive to everything around him. Sean is brutality personified, he pisses everybody off because he doesn't like anybody or anything, and then there's me who's a bit musical and a bit of a lad.
James (1994)

We looked at ourselves while we were recording the album (Everything Must Go) and thought either we go for a Latino thing – put on as much weight as we can, grow beards and come back as Roberto Duran or Marlon Brando in fat phase, or go for something more simple. The only thing people got wrong was calling us the Littlewoods Manic Street Preachers. Sean was deeply offended by that, because everything he buys is Paul Smith or Katharine Hamnett.
Nicky (1997)

This phase of supposedly being the Band At C&A is fine by me. Except I've got my Harvey Nics charge card now. Pop down to the sales, pick up Armani jeans for £40.
Sean (1997)

In the past we would follow Nick on how the band looked. Like, the army stuff, that was just what Nick was wearing. The only time I felt uncomfortable was at the start, when there was all the androgyny. I just didn't have the bone structure, did I?
James (1997)

I remember Sean used to feel a bit awkward with the glam look as well. The camouflage he didn't mind, 'cos he could buy a lot of it. We'd get a pin-on badge and Sean would come in with a £180 Russian medal.
Nicky (1997)

If we were as big then as we are now, the four of us in camouflage could have put on the most scary, fantastic live show ever. I have this picture of us at Glastonbury in 1994 with balaclavas and Russian hats, thinking we were an army and we could take anyone on. We'll never feel like that again.
Nicky (1997)

We were rock's equivalent of the TSB. The band that likes to say 'yes'.
Nicky (1994)

I feel past it at 27, but I still try to make a semblance of an effort. It's up to a younger band. But I look around, and there are no bands out there who take any risks in the way they dress. It really disappoints me. It's either sports gear or black casual shirts. With us it was always, 'come on Mooro, get this fucking blouse on'.
Nicky (1997)

When you're playing the songs off The Holy Bible to a really partisan audience, and you're all dressed up in military gear like a fucking soldier, it makes you feel more aggressive. I still feel like doing it. I don't feel like smashing things up so much anymore, because... my back's bad, and I'm just a bit older.
Nicky (1997)

You could say that I had an eating problem because if I ate too much, and I was drinking, I got all puffed up and blotchy. And I'm too vain to be like that. I couldn't handle looking in a mirror. All is vanity.
Richey (1994)

In the last year I've been doing loads of exercise. I do about 1,500 sit-ups every day. I do some weights as well. I take them on tour with me. It's about trying to control my body, to eat less and get fit. I want a flat stomach, I want a six pack, I want a stomach like Brad Pitt. I'm incredibly vain.
Richey (1994)

Richey once dressed up as a semen for Rag Week, and painted himself all white. He soon learned the error of his ways.
Nicky (1994)

If you're hopelessly depressed like I was, dressing up is just the ultimate escape… nothing could excite me except attention, so I'd dress up as much as I could. Outrage and boredom just go hand in hand.
Nicky (1993)

We're going to die young and leave good-looking corpses.
Nicky (1992)

What's heavenly? Pure rock'n'roll, dolphins, waking up and realising we're the sexiest, most intelligent, hateful rock'n'roll band in the whole world.
Richey (1991)

We are the scum factor of the Mondays meets the guitar overload of Five Thirty/Ride while killing Birdland with politics.
Richey (1989)

We all decided that from the start, me and Richey can't write music but we can write lyrics and look pretty tarty. Richey's the spirit of the band.
Nicky (1991)

Every morning Richey would wake up with a really bad hangover after drinking a litre of vodka. Then he'd go to the gym, exercise, swim, do lots of weights, have a jacket potato with all his grapes, and then not eat anything else for the rest of the day until he started drinking again. He knew full well that in the rock'n'roll world it's either the food or the booze in order to keep one's figure. Not both.
Nicky (1993)

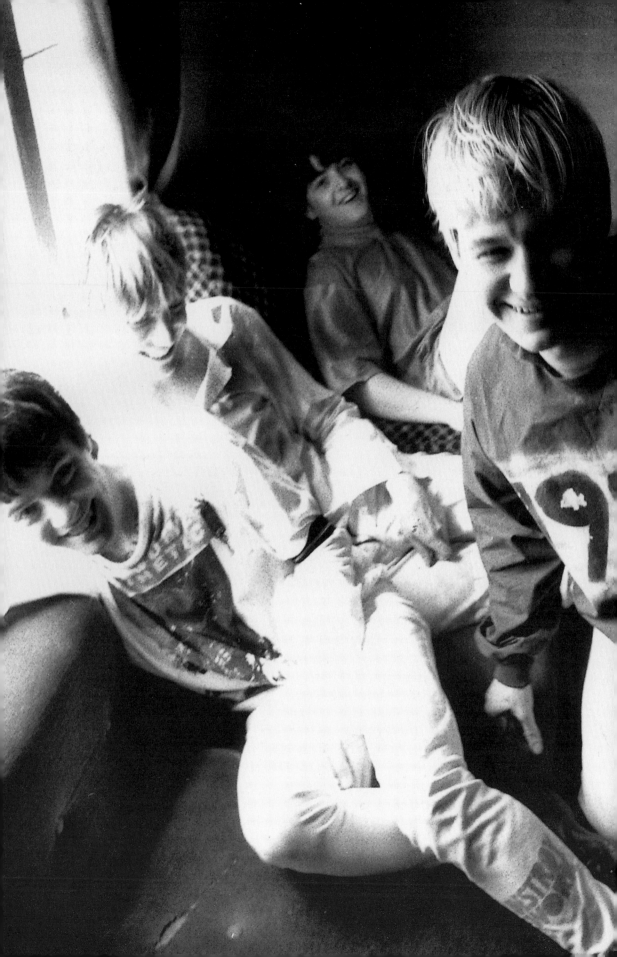

Generation Terrorists

We are just another band in the racks, but with more intelligence.
Richey (1991)

I'm just interested in getting three Number 1 singles, pissing off to America and making the greatest rock album of all time.
Nicky

One of our best abilities is to arrive at the same realm of consciousness at the same time, the same mood. That's the way it's got to be. I've got to justify what I do. Just being an entertainer or a singer-guitarist isn't enough. We've got to be a band that has a collective consciousness.
James (1996)

You can maybe ignore our songs but when we walk down the street and you see our song titles on our chests you've got to think something.
Richey

The more you achieve, the more blasé most bands get...*Generation Terrorists* went gold in Britain, sold 100,000, but that wasn't an achievement to us because we said we were going to sell 16 million. It does make a better band by putting that continual pressure on yourselves. We're always striving for something more.
Nicky

In the band at the moment, it's a matter of giving ourselves some human grace, the chance to show emotion other than disdain or hate and not be ashamed of it. Breathe a bit more. I think we've survived under a heavy load of self-censorship.
James (1996)

We've been accused of slagging off every band there is, and we've been told to stop. But our statement is that we hate every other band. We're not interested in them. That's all we can say. I've got no respect for any other band in the world.
Nicky (1991)

When we do interviews for Japanese magazines they get all upset because they want us to be all obnoxious and we aren't really. We actually get faxes from the record company in Japan saying, please tell the Manic Street Preachers to spit on people. It's just sad. That's what people want. It's pathetic.
Richey (1992)

We read all the books about the Rolling Stones and Kiss and now the saddest thing is that we do all the things that every other band does but we get no pleasure from it. It's not glamorous, it's not exciting, it's not like being in a Who documentary at all. We had millions of groupies in Cardiff last night, but it's not as good as reading about it in the *Kiss On Tour* book.
Richey (1992)

If we looked like we felt then we would have come onstage like Joy Division. We had to make a massive effort to be a glamorous band, because inside we know we're not particularly glamorous really.
Nicky

Seeing Mick Jagger jumping about doing 'Jumping Jack Flash' was the most important thing in our lives. Isn't that pathetic? I'd like to do something worthwhile like Nick's brother who helps people who are dying of cancer – but none of us could ever do anything like that because we'd always be whining 'Ooh, I want to watch a video, put the telly on'. We just feel sad there are no groups like the Rolling Stones any more. We are here at the complete death of rock culture
Richey (1992)

Neil Kinnock is our MP. His constituency house is in the same street as James' – and he's such a tosser. Party politics always seemed irrelevant to us. We got obsessed with cultural politics, it seemed more relevant; the real issues

like how futile life is, how fucked-up modern society is. In terms of music, we went back and rediscovered the great bands. Everything else seemed boring and worthless.
Richey (1991)

Even the bands from the past that we love – the Who, the Stones, the Pistols, the Clash – the way all of them turned out in the end was disillusioning, a let-down. We'll never let that happen.
Richey (1991)

We still read the music papers from cover to cover. On Wednesday that's all we do. That's all we've ever done.
Richey (1991)

We just totally despise people like Kingmaker, and think we should say that. Bands deserve to be exposed if they're so redundant, lyrically inept, ugly… and that's what those bands are.
Nicky (1991)

The zeitgeist of this year in general is fucking death and destruction.
Nicky (1994)

I still think Richey carving '4 Real' into his arm was a magnificent gesture. That's just the way we are, unfortunately. At the time it mattered so much to us, being in a band; that's what Richey felt he could do to express it.
Nicky (1994)

I think the bloke from Kula Shaker (Crispian Mills) talks some utter crap, but at least you can laugh. I like (Cast's) John Power: I think he's a bit of an angel, but he does talk some bollocks.
Nicky (1996)

I've never benefited from having a conversation with another band in my life. I'm not interested in being pally with other groups.
James (1993)

I'm not going to pretend that I'm converted to dance culture, because I find a lot of it extremely lazy. They call rock musicians Luddites, but they can't even pick up a pen and write lyrics half the time.
Nicky (1996)

I fucking hate the Beastie Boys. It's so much emphasis put on the quality of a sound loop. If you talked like that in rock about a guitar sound, everyone would take the piss out of you, but people will wax lyrical about Beck no end.
Nicky (1996)

I find Suede's keyboard player (Neil Codling) a bit odd. Everyone's supposed to fancy him, but I can't see Ocean Colour Scene fans fancying him. They'd probably want to batter him.
Nicky (1996)

I absolutely despise John Spencer Blues Explosion with a vengeance. He signed to his major label and tried to lose some weight and look cool, but it's corporate Nick Cave with a pretence of having some kind of edge. He reckons he's incorporating hip-hop: bollocks! That's like saying just because we get re-mixed by the Chemicals, we're bastions of the fucking dancefloor.
Nicky (1996)

That fucking Björk remix album: how did journalists ever fall for her? Talentless piece of shit. But you can't even say that because (then-boyfriend) Goldie will probably beat you up.
Nicky (1996)

Nick Cave is allowed to get away with writing songs about smashing a woman's head in with a brick – but if a band like us did it, there'd be even more outcry.
Nicky (1996)

As far as British music is concerned, there will never be another band as dangerous as us. Bands are too friendly. I detest every musician I've ever met.
Nicky (1994)

No band faces hysteria any more, unless they're Take That. Brett Anderson could walk around Brighton and no-one would bother. People don't care any more.
Nicky (1994)

The first thing I ever said in an interview with the music press was 'we're gonna set fire to ourselves on *Top Of The Pops*'. You don't say things like that for shock, there's some sort of sub-conscious. I do worry about ourselves, as people.
Nicky (1996)

Beck is vastly overrated. Typical maverick US lyrics that pretend to be intelligent, but deep down mean absolutely fuck-all. I know he's very credible, but I just don't see it. He's got a good haircut and that's about it.
Nicky (1997)

This year's the first time I've actually met people in other bands. It's hard to avoid it when you're at festivals. Before, I've always completely secluded myself. But when you actually meet people, I can't bring myself to go out in the press the next week and take the piss out of them. I couldn't live with myself if I couldn't say it to their face. Whereas before it was all right because I'd just say summat, and never see these people.
Nicky (1997)

We always knew we were going to fuck up. Everyone knew we were going to fuck up. We were really saying, 'Let's forget notions of contradiction. When it comes to bands, everyone fucks up, everyone lets you down'. Contradictions are meaningless, there's nothing to betray.
Nicky (1994)

Right now I don't want to go out, I don't want to make any friends. All I want to do is make enemies. I've never felt this much contempt for everyone and everything in my entire fucking life. I don't feel the need for anyone to like me anymore. Jesus, it's hard enough to like myself.
Nicky (1994)

We've reached a point now where we feel as if we've prostituted ourselves so fucking much, just given and given and given, that we've given everything away, and we've got absolutely fucking nothing left of our own. And we played up to that, you know – 'culture sluts'. But these things catch up with you.
Nicky (1994)

I know what I think made us special. But spiritually for others, I haven't got a clue. Except maybe… too much truth?
Nicky (1996)

We will always hate Slowdive more than Adolf Hitler.
Richey (1991)

Breakfast is always sad on a Wednesday because the music press arrives.
Richey (1992)

We're banning Charlatans fans from our gigs because they all have moustaches.
Nicky (1992

In this season of goodwill, let's hope Michael Stipe goes the same way as Freddie Mercury pretty soon.
Nicky (1992)

The Stipe comment is the one I could be pushed into showing a morsel of regret about. Otherwise, we have a *Murder On The Orient Express* mentality. We all willingly step forward to stab the corpse.
James (1996)

I've got nothing against Michael (Stipe) at all. I'm just all for bitchin' in music.
Nicky (1992)

Everybody knows that the Happy Mondays made some fucking great records, but we could never say that, because it was our blinkered Pol Pot period, and we didn't like what they were supposed to represent.
Richey (1993

Somebody should build some more by-passes over this shithole (Glastonbury).
Nicky (1994)

All the best bands get really fucked up… we're not saying there's anything glamorous in getting fucked up, we're not saying there's anything glamorous in being dead, but there's nothing glamorous in having a 20-year career either. That's even more sick.
Nicky (1994)

Some 'Cult Of Richey' disciples just won't be happy unless everybody else in the band becomes ill. I'm not willing to fall into that trap.
Nicky (1995)

The only good thing about New York is that it killed off John Lennon.
Nicky (1992)

As long as there are a few people who understand, it's okay. That's why we never minded doing teenage magazines like *Smash Hits* which some bands refuse to do. I just find that incredibly patronising. I know when I was 14, music was the only thing I cared about.
James (1994)

At the time most journalists seemed to be public school drop-outs. You could pick them off one by one. They'd been put in public school and they'd fucked up because they weren't very intelligent. And we'd come along we were very bright, we'd stress the fact that we were educated and they didn't want to know. They wanted to make us their playthings.
Nicky

The only beautiful thing about London is McDonalds.
Richey (1991)

We get compared to the greatest bands ever and are accused of being crap. If you start comparing the music journalists to the greatest writers ever, you soon see how shit they are too.
James (1991)

Music journalists don't even look good. I saw Andrew Collins on television and I nearly threw up. My God, he looked like a Pork Pie Dwarf with a pudding-bowl haircut… At least Nick Kent looked beautiful.
Nicky (1991)

When Steve Clarke of Def Leppard died, a man who'd written songs that sold 60 million or whatever, classically cool, why did he get about that much (holds up thumb and forefinger, millimetres apart) in the press? Yet when Shaun Ryder, talentless and brain-dead, has a baby, he gets a page. Why does he deserve it?
Nicky (1991)

30 is a very desperate age; rock music is being done by people in their 30s for teenagers. You get to 30 and look back and realise you've achieved nothing, you are nothing, and you've got nothing coming up.
Sean (1991)

Pride, Prejudice And Welshness

The only perfect circle on the human body is the eye. When a baby is born it's so perfect, but when it opens its eyes it's just blinded by the corruption and everything else is a downward spiral.
Richey

We didn't learn anything from other Welsh bands, just never to be remotely like them. It's really patronising, the way they suddenly decided to learn to speak the Welsh language, when they'd written songs about the bright lights of Mersey and Liverpool about two years before. And the Welsh language was never important to us at all. I mean, what's the point of resurrecting something that's completely dead? Dead culture doesn't interest us.
Richey (1993)

Most bands look forward to their homecoming gig. I don't expect roses and petals at my feet but the amount of grief we get here is non-stop. Anything from Welsh bands complaining about us not singing in Welsh to gangs of blokes pouring lager over me and saying 'What are you gonna do about that?' Tom Jones doesn't get this!
Richey

The working class is patronised a lot these days. Working-class imagery is taken by the middle-class people.
Nicky (1996)

I do want to get a place in Cardiff, but I feel I've got to live in London – for the band. It's the only way I can stay detached. If I went home I'd become obsessed with my own history. I remember so many things, good things that don't exist anymore. I get maudlin and lose all my energy. There's a transience in London that keeps me ticking over.
James (1996)

There's an awful lot of white British kids who have never really gone hungry, always had a roof to live under but at the same time are desperately unhappy. It's not total poverty, just a poverty of ideas.
Richey

All great art is always massive and well-known. No great art is reclusive. That's why Van Gogh sells for £50 million.
Nicky (1991)

Computer games are much more exciting than bands. We had our Sega Megadrive when we were down the studio making our record *(Generation Terrorists)* and we were spending hours a day playing on it because it's so engrossing. You feel involved, which you can't feel with music anymore. It's much better than travelling in the rain to see a band. But it's so sad that the best human minds on the planet are just trying to invent characters like Sonic The Hedgehog.
Richey (1992)

A Gibson Les Paul was one of the only things I'd ever longed for. I had it for two concerts and then I smashed it up. On impulse really. I did regret it after, I've got to admit. Then I got another Gibson and I smashed that up. I did feel quite ashamed because it was like my father's accumulated wage for about four weeks. I was just showing off and I felt ashamed.
James (1992)

Where we come from, to see any band you like, you normally have to travel quite a way. Faced with a choice between doing that, or staying home and blowing up planet after planet, then I know what most people would do. But the idea that video games are killing rock'n'roll is misleading. They exist with each other. They're different mediums.
Richey

You get these fans called Jeremy. They think they're being rebellious because they wear smelly jeans and have matted hair. Then you get the Welsh ones who think you're trying to do something important for Wales. We've never said good things about where we come from. All we've said is 'We're from Wales, from a town where there's nothing to do.' We've never felt any sense of pride in where we come from. Of course, if we were Irish and saying this, we'd be crucified for it.
James (1992)

Right now it seems the hierarchy of British pop – Oasis, Damon – wants to be seen with Tony Blair. We're still the band who'd rather be seen with Arthur Scargill. It kind of makes me feel good that we're still out of step. It's a good Manics trait.
Nicky (1997)

I have discovered my Welshness much more over the past few years. My greatest ambition is to do a film script on Owain Glyndwr, who was kind of Wales' William Wallace. He defeated the English and gave Wales self-rule. Anthony Hopkins could play him in old age, but I'm not sure who would do him when he was young.
Nicky (1997)

I'm proud that the Welsh were the last miners to go back to work. Quite cool.
Nicky

When we started the idea of Welsh music was like the Ivory Coast at the Olympics: one bloke carrying the flag and one walking behind. Now there's more of us and we can carry our banner with pride.
Sean (1997)

We realised the four of us were very different from the outside world. We're very proper. We did believe the Welsh thing; get an education.
Nicky (1996)

I think there's a lot of people who feel uncool, and they realise that getting into dance music is the one thing that can make them cool. I think that's true for a lot of people, whether it's dodgy old punks from the 1970s who were in shit bands and now they make dance music, or they're young kids putting 'Technics' or 'Kenwood' on their bags.
Nicky (1996)

I don't blame Liam for walking out on Oasis's US tour. It isn't like Oasis cancelled their tour and ruined our schedule. I think it's brilliant that they did it. And the MTV thing was brilliant, I thought they out-fronted everyone. It did stir my emotions quite a bit, and it does make you feel a little too much of a Brit, but I can't help that. I always see music in terms of a sporting contest.
Nicky (1996)

Sexual politics have never been on my agenda. Richey might have been more interested in that. Basically, I think men are cunts and women are fine. Ninety five per cent of violent crime is still caused by men. Men are nastier. I do get on better with blokes, but I know deep down we're all pretty… dodgy.
Nicky (1996)

Perhaps I'm xenophobic in the sense that I find it very hard to fit in in other countries. Then again, I find it equally hard to fit in in Wales sometimes.
Nicky (1994)

We were a Welsh rock band and in the eyes of some people then that was the very worst thing in the whole world. We were totally a product of our environment, but we had to prove we weren't the Alarm.
James (1996)

I'm not into tribalism any more. I'm into oneness. We're too small in Wales to divide any more. There's three times as many people in London as the whole of Wales.
Nicky (1997)

At the start we never went around wearing Welsh credentials. Richey was really paranoid about ever coming across as Welsh. He always called it the Neil Kinnock factor. I've become more conscious of it lately. I've started to support the Welsh rugby side. *Vanity Fair* interviewed Sharon Stone recently: they asked her to name her favourite Irish author and she said Dylan Thomas. Things like that

wouldn't have annoyed me before, but they really do now.
Nicky (1997)

When you've got nothing, you've got something pure that no one can take away. As soon as you've got something, some cunt's gonna come and take it off you.
James (1994)

For me the greatest figure in British history is still Nye Bevan. It just fucking sickens me that people have been conned into believing that you can't think in terms of class any more. As soon as working-class people lose their sense of belonging, they lose all their humility, and you get a classless society in the worst possible sense.
James (1994)

In Wales the women are as bored as the men, but the men will go out to the pub and beat the shit out of everyone else. The women will stay at home and concentrate on surviving.
Richey (1992)

The media are so into this idea of 'Generation X' at the moment. This concept of teenage discontent. But they're just celebrating these kids saying, 'Ooh, we've always had money, but the second they took the spoon out of our mouths we decided maybe we never really liked our life after all and – hey, maybe we won't get a job'. They'd never publish anything by some scummy, junked-up bastard from Manchester, they're only concerned with willing under-achievers from the upper middle classes.
James (1994)

I'm never going to lose touch with myself, or with where I came from. The only destructive force in my life is alcohol, and even that never got me into trouble, it just made me put on weight.
James (1996)

Where I come from I've seen violence, I've been in stomach-churning fights, bones broken and everything, but even that doesn't turn my stomach as much as some of the things I see in London. The perpetuation of certain privileges, certain forms of so-called intelligence… that really horrific provincial violence seems more understandable.
James (1996)

One thing I'm proud of is that where I come from, throughout the whole mining area, every colliery in every town gave money to build an institute, with a library, with complete access for free, which was a way of keeping your class, but having access to education and learning – that's why I ended up at university. The fact is now, almost every one of those institutes has been destroyed. So now you've got this pit-bull terrier working class, completely without pride, and you'd be very naive to think the working class had done that to themselves. It's down to an actual plan by the Conservative government to destroy the working class.
Nicky (1996)

You go and see a film like *Seven* and you realise that most people can't become what they want these days, and the one thing you can become is a killer. It's the easiest thing in the fucking world.
Nicky (1996)

We're not the fucking Senseless Things. We don't want to return to some supposed golden day like they do. You hear bands like that and they talk as if now is useless and everything in 1977 was so great. We're now. All you can do with the past is to never want to be like it. 'Cos the past has created what we're living in now, and we're not happy, so it must've failed.
Richey (1991)

We're not left wing but we do have roots in Situationism and stuff, and when we formed the band, the miners' strike was going on on our doorsteps. So when you

listen to 'Archives Of Pain' *(The Holy Bible)*, a very right-wing song, it shows how fucked up and confused our times are. And it shows that we're still arrogant and unafraid enough to make judgements, even miscalculated ones.
James (1994)

Everyone likes Happy Mondays 'cos when the working class dance, it means nothing except prole fashion. The Stone Roses seem to understand the working class, but only in interviews. No one is speaking for people like us.
Richey (1991)

People we met in London would never like the idea of meeting a girl in a pub and having a bag of chips and a fuck in the bus stop on the way home. That's something ordinary, working-class people do all the time. We'd do that; we wouldn't check into a hotel – it'd be, 'Stop here a minute, I want my dick sucked'. That's the scum factor.
Richey (1990)

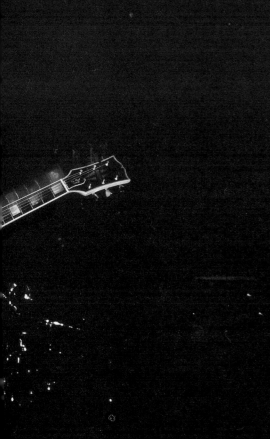

I've never thought a band could ever do anything that's important. It can change individuals, it can create a common ground for important issues, but in terms of actually doing something, changing the economic infrastructure, it's not gonna do that. It never has done.
Richey (1993)

We are the scum that remind people of misery. When we jump on the stage it's not rock'n'roll cliché but the geometry of contempt. We don't display our wounds, we shove them in people's faces. We are the decaying flowers in the playground of the rich. We are young, beautiful scum, pissed off with the world.
Richey (1989)

Wipe out aristocracy now, kill, kill, kill. Queen and country dumb flag scum. We are drowning in manufactured ego fucking. Boredom bred the thoughts of throwing bricks.
Richey (1989)

New Art Riot was one of the first slogans we used to spray everywhere. It was our most grey, political and dogmatic time. We read *Marxism Today* and carried the *Communist Manifesto* everywhere, and we went through a naive phase of putting Lenin and Che Guevara posters on our walls. But it was the height of Madchester – a barren time for lyrics – so we were determined to say something.
Nicky (1993)

We've never been the Trade Unionists of rock. We know that we could never reach as many people as we wanted, unless it was on a major (label). We were willing prostitutes.
James (1991)

We came to feel we were part of a culture that didn't exist anymore. We wanted to believe in something and couldn't find anything to believe in. We wanted to attach some new-found intelligence or theory to the place and the class we came from. But we were always confused, always contradictory, always very suspicious. Suspicious of the smell of the burning martyr.
James (1996)

Language has always been our weapon. Our lyrics are getting stronger and if you hurt a couple of 'nice' people along the way, or offend them, then that's necessary.
James (1991)

I was listening to Gene on the radio talking about 'Sleep Well Tonight' and the singer was going, 'Oh, we've taken all this video footage of people spilling out of pubs and beating themselves up and it's so terrible', and I thought, 'What the fuck do you expect them to do when they've been working in a factory for 20 years? These people will start a revolution – not the Martin Rossiters of this world who just stay in reading Morrissey lyrics all their lives. It's really wrong to patronise these people.
Nicky (1996)

METROPOLITAN POLICE SERVICE

PNC W/M No:

Form 584 (C)   **Station Copy**

Please use BLOCK CAPITALS/Do NOT fold
*Delete as appropriate

Send photograph if available to
B14 with Form 584. Original
will be returned after copying

Stn. Ref. No: 584/21

Class class: ~~person missing~~ person, body found
absentee from care, mental absconder, hospel

*LIMITED/ENQUIRY   Station: HARROW ROAD

Surname:	Forenames:	Male/Female/Unknown	DOB (if not known give age)
EDWARDS	RICHARD	Male	22 12 67

Ethnic appearance: (White European) Dark European/Negroid/Asian/Oriental/Arab/Doubt   Height: 5 ft 8 ins

Alias: —

Birthplace: BLACKWOOD

Nationality: WELSH

Warning signals: (drugs, suicidal, depressed, violent, etc) ON ANTIDEPRESSANTS.

Marks, scars, tattoos, physical peculiarities:
SEVERAL TATTOOS
ROSE 'USELESS GENERATION
ON LEFT ARM.

Habits/other characteristics:
(smokes, drinks, etc.)
SMOKES

Date of incident:	1²95 0700	Date of report:	2 2 95

Cross Ref., other person(s) involved:

Build: (slim) medium/heavy/other

Hair: colour SHAVED/SHAVED length ____ style

*Beard/moustache/wig/other:

Eyes: colour BROWN   *glasses/contact lenses

Complexion: PALE

Clothing—include full description and colour:

Jumper   N/K.

Trousers

Skirt

Topcoat

Jacket Further tattoos - 2 ornate tattoos on shoulders (attempt but fades N/K).

Shirt

Footwear

Other

Jewellery: —

Address from which missing: LONDON EMBASSY HOTEL

Home address if different: 6 ANSON CT, SCHOONER WAY, ATLANTIC WHARF, CARDIFF

Circumstances: Subject is a member of a band and was staying in London embassy hotel with another band member before flying to USA on business. Subject was seen by hotel staff leaving hotel on 1²95 at 0700 + has not been seen since. His passport is missing but all his belongings are still in his hotel room. Subject has made a previous suicide attempt + is taking anti-depressants. Date/time last seen: 1²95 0700

School or Occupation: MEMBER OF POP BAND

Mental absconders: Order under 5   MHA 19   NOT to be arrested after

Care Order: To   Social Services

at

INFORMANT Name

Address 8 P...

...BRIDGE

Publicity authorised

Time 1009

...6288.

ACTION REFER...

Checks PNC

MSS To B14/86(4) S...

Transferred to:

Supervising...

CANCELLATION B14...

Supervising Of...

M.P.91

Time 1120

Time

Time

From Despair...

I suppose it was a gradual decline that led (Richey) to seeking treatment, but when he was at home he seemed reasonably happy and it was only later that we realised there was something seriously wrong.
Graham Edwards, Richey's father

When Richey's car was found on the Severn bridge we had to think… not so much about splitting up, but simply the prospect of everything being so dreadful. We were just frozen in disbelief. That's the closest we came without it being a literal 'splitting up' situation. There was no policy meeting, the only policy was to immediately cancel the US tour on the spot. It would have been pretty bad if Richey's body had been found while we were on tour.
Nicky (1996)

In the end Richey is one of those people who will always do the opposite of what you tell him.
James

Up until Richey's car was found I thought there was a good chance he'd turn up. After that I thought either he was dead or he wouldn't turn up for a long long time. I was in Wales when he went missing, so I rushed down to the flat and waited for him and he had been there by all accounts, because he dropped something off. But he never came. We started phoning hotels, asked every one in the country whether they had a Richard Edwards staying. And we found one in Swansea and thought we'd got him. I was just about to go down and it turned out to be just some businessman. After the car was found we thought, whatever he'd done, he wants to do it. If he's happy, good luck to him.
Nicky (1996)

If you have a body, you can let it flood out. Anger and grief. But we were just… suspended. Although the hope is still there, so is the dread. If I get a phone call and it's a wrong number, or the person just puts the phone down, it can ruin your whole week.
Nicky (1996)

There was the possibility Richey just didn't like us any more. That was a real blow, and that was the only time I wish he'd left some kind of note saying, 'Boys, it's for the best. But I still love you'. The fact he just disappeared is very upsetting, and I know that's selfish.
Nicky (1996)

I wonder whether Richey felt he had to justify himself. The lyrics on *The Holy Bible* were so harrowing that a lot of the press would say, 'How can you justify these records unless you top yourself afterwards?'.
Nicky (1996)

There are two very obvious things which have befallen us this year which have made me very aware of how things can be snatched away from you. I'm getting a bit weary of the arbitrary nature of life. I can't help thinking, 'Richey, if you could just have held on a little longer, things might have been a lot different. Maybe then you could have had all these things you wanted. You might have been happy'.
James (1996)

I wanted to go to Australia after Richey disappeared, but I ended up in Torquay for three days. Rock'n'roll, eh?
Nicky (1996)

For all we know he could have gone insane. The morning he left, for all we know, he could have gone mad.
Nicky (1996)

I'm superstitious and it did feel like a very scary, self-fulfilling prophecy. We made our own beds and we were always in love with rock myths. I mean, I still love Joy Division more than New Order.
James (1996)

I was adrift. Suddenly the focus of my life for the last six years was gone. I'd get up, make some tea, walk around, go out, get pissed with my mates and then do it all over again.
James (1996)

It was in the last six months that he really deteriorated. I could feel something was wrong. He'd call me late at night and talk about *Apocalypse Now* or *Naked* for two hours, trying to get some sort of idea across, and he just couldn't.
Nicky (1995)

If Richey doesn't want to come back, then that's fine. But we just want him to give us a call or send us a postcard.
Nicky (1995)

Rachel (Richey's sister) wrote to every monastery she could think of, and they wrote back saying they couldn't say. So he could easily just be living a quiet life somewhere.
Nicky (1995)

Everyone feels sorry for us right now. I think it might be a honeymoon period. I feel sorry that it took Richey to go missing before some people would accept us.
Nicky (1996)

Doctors keep saying, 'you've got to accept it, he's dead'. But I don't think anyone can accept someone's dead without a body.
Nicky (1997)

Deep down it's my gut feeling that he's alive. But that's not based on any logical evidence. I just try to tell myself that he'd done what he wanted to.
Nicky (1996)

When you're young you're bored and pissed off. Life seems futile. It does to us, even now.
Richey

...To Where?

People see us on stage, see me smiling, see us selling albums and having hits and they think we've forgotten. We haven't. We keep it to ourselves. We're willing to talk about Richey in interviews, but it's only between ourselves and with my wife that the real emotion comes out. That's when we really talk.
Nicky (1996)

Splitting up was perhaps a possibility right up until the first time we practised together (after Richey's disappearance).
Sean (1996)

We practised where we've always done it, an absolute shithole in Cardiff. We didn't walk in and burst out crying. We're not drama queens. We're too self-conscious for that.
Nicky (1996)

In a way, it was just like the very first rehearsal. We were apprehensive and unsure of what would happen. It wasn't like we looked at each other and said, 'Hey, it's still there... the magic'. It was just like normal. After 20 minutes we went shopping.
Sean (1996)

Between the three of us we can still be very sarcastic and take the piss about the whole thing, and that helps. It's the New Order school of thought: 'Ian Curtis was a twat 'cos he ruined our American tour'.
Nicky (1996)

Before Richey went missing he photocopied a whole file of 60 lyrics and gave a copy to each of us. But we haven't used any of those. The four or five songs we have used on the album were done before. It's funny how I've been written out of the story. Admittedly on *The Holy Bible* Richey wrote 70 per cent of the words. But up until then it had been 50:50, so it wasn't that difficult for us to move forward without Richey's lyrics.
Nicky (1996)

I'd just got married and moved into my new house, and I didn't want to write about death camps, so I'd amassed quite a stockpile of my own stuff anyway. There was a kind of temptation to break completely with the past and not use any of Richey's lyrics, but in the end it feels quite elegiac really.
Nicky (1996)

We played at the Hacienda – the first time we'd played a small gig since Richey disappeared. In the old days, Wire would bump into me on stage and I'd shoot Richey a look: 'What is he like?'. On Friday I looked over and there was no one there. I thought, 'What the fuck did I do that for?'. Apart from that it was strange. There were a few heavily dramatised tears being shed down the front.
James (1996)

We've sat down and discussed whether to record or not at great length, among ourselves and with Richey's family, and basically decided we would have a go. We've been rehearsing regularly for the last few months and have over 20 new songs, which have been written over the past year. The last six months have been very difficult for us, but we feel ready to start recording.
Nicky (1995)

How can I put myself in competition with Richey when he was one of my best mates? I'm not gonna go, 'We're gonna be bigger than ever'. You don't compete with your friends on that level.
James (1996)

(Fans) want to believe that he was perpetually tortured, and any kind of ordinariness they just don't want to see. They'll never believe that Richey and me played cricket for hours on end. The last year of being in the band he definitely did go downhill. We got one letter which said 'Why didn't you talk to him?' And I spent more time in my life talking to Richey and trying to understand him than I have done with any other person. He made my life a misery sometimes, because I was just worrying about him all the time.
Nicky

Two months ago I was out having a drink in London and someone says to me, 'How can you be out having a drink? If I was you, I know I'd be in my room, chopping myself up by proxy for Richey'.
James (1996)

I think it's good that we've kept certain memories to ourselves, because that keeps that sort of bond there. It doesn't become a myth. For us… it's still a bloke. I think it's really important that we keep hold of that.
Nicky (1997)

'Yes' is one of the band's favourite songs, it really is. James finds it impossible to sing live. It may be in the third person, about a prostitute, but it's so personal to Richey, he says, 'I can't do that live. I don't care how much I love that song'. It's weird being on stage when you've got these fucking myriad emotions going through your mind, that's what I usually forget when I'm playing.
Nicky (1997)

When your best friend was a genius, you don't want to throw away everything he stood for, just like that.
Nicky (1996)

The hardest thing is trying to speak on his behalf for fans' sakes. You get so paranoid, having to watch what you say. And then there's always the fear that he'll be reading it somewhere with a big beard, thinking, 'You twat'.
Nicky (1996)

I've tried to blank it out, to a certain degree. I won't give anybody the illusion that I'm sitting there waiting, 'cos we've all nearly fucked ourselves up over it and I've developed some kind of immunity towards it. I'd rather be shocked than wait on something now. Because I can't wait around any more.
James (1995)

The time you'd notice it was when we'd be in Nicky's room, socialising, and suddenly there'd be a lull in the conversation and we'd all realise that was the point Richey would have come up with one of his Richey-isms.
James (1995)

I remember the introduction to 'From Despair To Where' (at the Hacienda in Manchester), looking over to where Richey would have been standing, swigging at a bottle of whisky, and there was no one there. And when we came offstage I virtually had a breakdown. I was just crying hysterically for about three hours, like a twat. The first time I'd been able to cry since the day they found his car.
Nicky (1995)

The success of *Everything Must Go* is tainted by the knowledge that it's not the four of us enjoying it together.
James (1996)

The album isn't a goodbye to Richey. We could never say goodbye. He was my best friend. We talk about him all the time between ourselves. It's easier to live with now because we're getting busy again, but you still wake up every morning and think about him.
Nicky (1996)

What am I supposed to do? I loved him, and so did Nicky, and so did Sean… I can't sit in my room forever with the curtains closed being a cold fish. It's then that it's been really difficult to stop myself getting really violent.
James (1996)

We decided to carry on in April (1995) after two months of waiting by the phone and feeling really ill and exhausted. We were really paralysed and unable to do anything. We thought we'd been so close, and in the end we couldn't do anything for him. It's sad to think that perhaps he didn't like you.
Nicky (1995)

We did consider changing the name and starting over again…and we probably would have done if we knew he was dead. It would be more like a Joy Division/New Order thing then.
Nicky

The Music

Singles

'Motown Junk' (1991, on Generation Terrorists)

It's a hate song. It's just a blur of hatred, a constant tirade. Everything in our lives had been one long let-down.
Nicky (1991)

It was the starting point for us really. That was the first time we ever really felt like a band, the first time we created a record we could live with. We had people around us who understood exactly what we were trying to say and how we wanted to say it. Then we signed to Sony.
James (1994)

'Motorcycle Emptiness' (1992, on Generation Terrorists)

The record company never even released it in America – they didn't want it on the album 'cos they said it was too AOR. So our dreams were shattered straight away 'cos that was our universal song. If anything could do it, that could.
Nicky (1996)

'Theme From M*A*S*H'

We chose it because it reminded us of a very gloomy time in our lives. It was Number 1 when there was a Musicians' Union strike and no *Top Of The Pops*, which essentially meant there was no music on TV at all.
Richey (1992)

We just went into a little demo studio in Cardiff and did it in a day. We just kept playing it over and over until we got it right. It cost us 80 quid to do the whole thing.
Richey (1992)

I couldn't really care less about being a Top 10 chart star, the important thing was just to do a good job and make some money for the Spastics Society. I was pleased it didn't drop down the charts after the first week. The fact that it went up in the second week was a bigger thrill than going straight in at Number 9.
Richey (1992)

'Roses In The Hospital' (1993, on *Gold Against The Soul*)

It's just about the idea of something beautiful in a decaying place. It's about people who hurt themselves in order to concentrate, or just to feel something.
Richey

'Little Baby Nothing' (1994, on *Generation Terrorists*)

When we met Traci Lords and she came over, we just talked to her about the lyrics. At the time we were getting misrepresented 'cos of Richey's arm and everything, and she was just saying, 'you know, I keep coming round and people will say I'm a porn star. Whereas, if I was a man, people would think I'm great, I'm a celebrity, I get to be me'. I think she completely understood the song at the end.
Nicky (1993)

'Faster' (1994, on *The Holy Bible*)

I had more to do lyrically with 'Faster'. It's not a post-modern nightmare, it's more a voyeuristic insight into how our generation has become obliterated with sensations. We could deal with things but we prefer to blank them out so that virtually every atrocity doesn't have that much impact any more.
Nicky (1994)

Frankly, a lot of it is Richey again, and I was always completely confused by it. But when he wrote it he told me it was about self-abuse. The opening line is 'I am an architect/they call me a butcher' – and of course, he's been carving into his arm and all that… I think it's the most confusing song on the album. I added some stuff about the regurgitation of 20th century culture. It's probably the first time we've written a song and not completely understood what we've written.
Nicky (1994)

'Revol' (1994, on *The Holy Bible*)

This song is not about revolution and it's not about fucking S*M*A*S*H and it's got fuck all to do with the Family Cat.
Nicky (1994)

All those lines like 'Brezhnev married into group sex' are just analogies really. It's trying to say that relationships in politics, and relationships in general, are failures. It's very much a Richey lyric, and some of it's beyond my head. He's saying that all of these revolutionary leaders were failures in relationships – probably because all his relationships have failed.
Nicky (1994)

'She Is Suffering' (1994, on *The Holy Bible*)

It's quite a simple song, both musically and lyrically. It's kind of like the Buddhist thing where you can only reach eternal peace by shedding every desire in your body. I think that the last line, 'Nature's lukewarm pleasure' is Richey's views on sex. I can't really explain it, but that's the way he sees it.
Nicky (1994)

'A Design For Life' (1996, on *Everything Must Go*)

'A Design For Life' reminds me of 'Motown Junk', one of our first singles. But that was the most claustrophobic, angry record, a once in a lifetime for us.

The difference is we got more ambitious and we changed. There are only certain moments when you can look into the abyss and dive in. Now we kind of look and step away.
Nicky (1996)

For 'A Design For Life' to sell 300,000 copies and start with the line 'Libraries gave us power' – I'm really proud. Because even Blur and Oasis… Well, 'Country House' is just Madness yob pop, and Oasis's lyrics are hardly the deepest. I do think that's something we can be really proud of.
Nicky (1997)

I feel slightly bitter-sweet. It taints it. Lyrically, there doesn't seem to be much to that song, but the lines are so concise. As soon as I got those words I thought, 'I've got to write the best tune ever'. This was one of the first times in a while when I read a lyric and it sent a tingle up my spine. To transfer that to a Number 2 position – that gives me a sense of fulfilment.
James (1996)

Along with 'Motorcycle Emptiness', it's become our universal song now. Wherever you go, people know it. The lyrical content is something that we're pretty proud of. Simple as that.
Nicky (1997)

I've done a bit of damage to the band – me being in London, a bit of a boy around town and stuff. And when I got those lyrics, I actually felt part of where I came from, for once. I actually felt the disillusionment which I'd deferred by getting pissed. That track actually put me back on track a tiny bit.
James (1996)

Albums

Generation Terrorists (1992)

With the confidence we have in this album we wouldn't be happy unless it sold 16 million.
Nicky

This album is everything we wanted it to be. Every lyric is totally uncensored. Every bit of music we ever wanted, we have.
Richey (1991)

It is a fucked-up album because we tried so hard to make some songs rock FM. No band in our position has ever tried to do that: write a six-minute epic depressive song ('Motorcycle Emptiness'). It'd be easier and more credible to make ten versions of 'Motown Junk'.
Nicky (1992)

The thing about Generation Terrorists was that the title was misunderstood. At the age of 10 or 12 everybody is full of some kind of optimism, yet by the time that they leave school they've given up on everything. In those five or six years your life has been dramatically changed and pretty much destroyed. That's what the title meant.
The whole point was to be hypocritical, to be false. All we wanted to do was to write better songs and find a better economy with words. We are improving all the time. Everybody knows the first album would've been better if we'd left out all the crap – but we wanted it to be a double, so nothing was left out.
Richey

It would be wrong to say we regretted it. We could have sold a lot more records if we'd done a debut album that was ten songs just like 'Motown Junk' and played the game a bit more carefully, but I prefer bands when they're messy and sprawling and epic, and they make mistakes.

We've made indie bands realise – even on the smallest level – that you can be stars again… that's all down to us. Musically and lyrically they're not gonna take anything from us. I know that – they're too scared.
Nicky

Gold Against The Soul (1993)

There's too much bluster. There's some great singles, but it's definitely not a masterpiece.
Nicky (1996)

The first album was more a statement of intent. This one is far more musical, more current. We were a little too scared to make a hash of things last time. But we don't like slagging off past records. It's like we're despising our fans for buying them.
James (1993)

The Holy Bible (1994)

It's not a party record. It's not 'Abba Gold', but there are a few basic home truths on it.
James (1994)

I really enjoyed how it confronts the audience, but it confronts us too. You play it on stage and you can feel Damien round the corner. It feels like handling a cursed chalice; you can feel the lesions breaking out all over your body.
James (1996)

We just wanted to make a statement that was anti-everything. But in the end it was too grim. It's one of those albums you won't play very often, but it's comforting that it's there nestling in your record collection somewhere.
Nicky (1996)

It's gothic with a small 'g'. It's not Cranes, but it is quite a morbid album. We've rejected our past in a lot of ways with this album. There's a bit of early Joy Division on it, and a few PIL basslines.
Nicky (1994)

You might think 'Yes' reads about prostitution, but it's the prostitution of what we've felt over the last three years. There's a line in there 'There's no part of my body that has not been used', and I think that might start with me and Richey having love bites on the first *NME* cover, then escalates to Richey or whoever sleeping with groupies to cutting yourself. It's like what Red Indians believe, that your soul is taken away when you're photographed constantly. It does get to a point where it feels like that.
Nicky (1994)

'Yes' is the song I find hardest to sing. It doesn't put a lump in my throat or anything, it just makes me feel that I can't do it justice. It makes me feel a bit futile, a bit cabaret.
James (1994)

'Die In The Summertime' has got one of the most frightening lines ever, where it goes 'A tiny animal curled into a quarter circle'. That really scares me. It's hard to explain some of these things without Richey being here.
Nicky (1994)

Everything Must Go (1996)

We're all glad the album's coming out when it is. I think it has a real summer side to it. We're very proud of it and I'm sure if Richey ever gets the chance to hear it, he'll feel the same.
Nicky (1996)

With the first album, we definitely did think we would sell a lot, and we always fell well below the expectations of what we thought an important band should sell. With *Everything Must Go*, in the way we talked about it, we were the most timid we'd ever been, because we were

very nervous. It was strange, because it was the most un-Manic we've been about an album, and then it was the most successful.
James (1997)

'Interiors' *(Everything Must Go)* is a tribute to the painter Willem de Kooning, who suffers from Alzheimer's disease. Apparently he's a hypochondriac – and, being one too, I can sympathise with him.
Nicky (1996)

Everything Must Go isn't exactly a feel-good album, but I think it's an album that soothes. With 'Enola/Alone' and 'Australia', people can grab hold of them because they're melancholic but also uplifting – everybody gets that kind of sad uplifting moment. It's raining, or you're pissed, but you're still kind of okay. I think that's what those two songs translate to. I knew 'Enola/Alone' had to be la-la-la, it had to be a Noel Gallagher structure and still have Manics traits in it.
Nicky (1997)

Every song is a good song. It's more Spectoresque, rather than rock, a lot of the time. It was my Brian Jones contribution to say 'get a harp'. My one musical idea in five years. And we've always been trying to get Sean to play the trumpet.
Nicky (1996)

Everything Must Go stands for getting rid of some of the baggage and learning that we have to break our own rules sometimes. This time we realised we couldn't make every album like an encyclopedia. Once upon a time we could never have done a song like 'Further Away', which is almost a love song. It's healthy do be able to do whatever we like without always having to think, 'Wait a minute, we're the Manic Street Preachers'.
James (1996)

'Elvis Impersonator' is all about Britain accepting crap American culture and putting it on a pedestal.
Nicky (1996)

I have to quote one of Richey's lyrics here and say that ours was a Pyrrhic victory. It felt like a relief more than anything else. We had success without compromising or riding on the back of any moments like Britpop, grunge or baggy. We were always outsiders, always deeply unfashionable. That hasn't really changed.
James (1996)

Friends And Relations

Since (manager) Philip (Hall) died we've taken each day as it comes. Philip's death was so arbitrary. At least Richey exercised some kind of control. But they were both slow declines. 'Enola/Alone' on the album *(Everything Must Go)* stems from that, from me looking at my wedding photos and seeing two people standing right by me who aren't around anymore.
Nicky (1996)

No one in my immediate family's ever died, so it was the first funeral I'd been too. Philip wasn't just a manager, unfortunately. We lived with him for virtually a year, he lent us about £45,000 before we got a deal, virtually financed us.
Nicky (1994)

Philip had a big impact on our lives. He was the first person that ever believed in our music; the first to respond to all the stupidly long letters we would send out to anyone we could think of. He said 'I'll come and see you do a gig in London'. We said we couldn't get a gig in London. So he drove down to see us in a crappy schoolroom.
Richey (1994)

We really had no notion of what Philip did, or how helpful he could be to us. We just thought he sounded like a person who could help us out. Within three months he'd become our manager, we escaped from Wales and the four of us slept on his floor in London for six months. He put up with a lot: by the time we'd signed to Sony he'd re-mortgaged his house for us. Even when we smashed our equipment up he never got pissed off – in fact he used to encourage it. He used to have a glint in his eye. He loved a good wind-up and at least before he died we'd repaid the faith he'd put in us by starting to become a successful band.
Nicky (1994)

Traci Lords is female power. We wanted her or Kylie on 'Little Baby Nothing' because at the time they were both women who were perceived as puppets. No one could imagine that they might have their own vision on how they wanted to be sold.
Richey (1992)

Traci Lords was the nicest American I've ever met, up until now.
Nicky (1993)

You know, I miss my dog Snoopy. He died two weeks ago. That's why I shaved my head… he was 17 years old. I've had him since I was little.
Richey (1995)

Over To You – The Manics From The Outside

(Richey) must have read books from day one while the rest of us were watching telly. He's very intelligent. I think he finds it difficult talking to people who aren't similarly educated. He'd sit there quoting things and I'd be nodding thinking, 'I don't know what you are talking about.'
Ian Ballard, Damaged Goods Records (who put out the 'New Art Riot' EP in 1990)

I signed the Manics, I suppose, because I went to see a gig in Guildford and I thought they were the most exciting thing I'd seen since the Clash in 1977… who I also signed. I just thought they were amazing, it's refreshing all the way through, even for an old fart like me.

They're no more anarchistic than anyone else of their age, or my age come to that. They have something to say, they're pissed off about where they live, they're pissed off about unemployment but they're not so pissed off that they can't enjoy themselves and express themselves. And that's what young people are meant to do.
Tim Bowen, Sony/Columbia Managing Director

When I first got into the Manics I had the same feeling I had with Public Enemy. They were just one of those bands that, if you were gonna get into them, you had to decide, you had to let them take you over. I don't think anybody else will ever make an album remotely like *The Holy Bible* ever again. It's so fucking awesome, it's the kind of album any lesser band would spend the rest of their career trying to live up to, or live down.
Martin Carr, the Boo Radleys

The culture of despair has given way to the culture of sympathy. The same shallow scum that once threw stones are now falling over themselves to salute the band's valiant Carrying On In The Face Of Loss.
Dickon Edwards, Orlando

Aren't Terrorvision the band who ran over one of their own fans? Good fucking idea. I can think of a few bands who should do that. The Manics, for instance.
Richard Parfitt, 60ft Dolls

Thing about the Manics is that they've become total pros. There's no ego to deal with, no bullshit and none of the mayhem that normally goes with life on the road.
Deptford Andy (long-standing roadie)

They look like someone doing the Clash in a school play.
Steve Hanley, the Fall

When I first met them, they were very Clash-based, and I helped them get that stereo guitar sound. They weren't particularly opinionated, they just bashed it down. They demoed about half the songs that later turned up on *Generation Terrorists*.

Nick and Richey didn't play on anything, James did all their parts. They never professed to being musicians. In fact, they never turned up for the 'Bored Out Of My Mind' session.

They were a good bunch of boys, really, even though they used to look really aggressive. If they owed me £20 for a session, the next time they came in they'd put it down on the table before anything else. You could trust them.
Glen Powell, Sound Bank Studios

I asked them whether I could put out a single, and after a couple of phone calls, they came round my house in Walthamstow to suss me out. Basically, I was being auditioned to see if I could do their single! We sat around playing video games, as you do. James and Richey did most of the talking – they were very straightforward and down to earth. They recorded the tracks at the Workshop in Redditch over two days. It was the only studio I knew about.
Ian Ballard

The Future

Live, we know we haven't reached the heights of excitement we had with Richey. the sound and the playing are good, but in terms of us looking at one another and knowing we could take on the world, change people's lives… we haven't regained that and without Richey, without the aura, perhaps we never will.
Nicky (1996)

One way or another, things will never be the same. It's looking over and not seeing Richey knocking back his ten vodkas. We'll never fill that gap. We'll never get another guitarist. James will never go over to that side of the stage.
Nicky (1996)

I couldn't be friends with him again. Just for the sake of us three. If it went off again, just imagine how much it would fuck you up. It's my biggest nightmare – what would I do if Richey turned up and wanted to know me again? It's really scary.
James (1996)

We're not going to use any more of Richey's lyrics. We only used them on this album *(Everything Must Go)* because he actually heard the songs. They were works-in-progress before he left. We wouldn't want to write a song without him hearing it in any shape or form. Maybe it'd be better to publish them in a little book. They're not like lyrics anyway, they're more like poems.
Nicky (1997)

I haven't got any ambition left at all any more. All that young man's ambition has been sucked out of me. I don't want to tour the world and change people's lives any more. I don't want to convert people to my way of thinking. All that's gone. It feels like we've given so much, and I just look back and think that maybe if we'd gone about things a different way we could all be sitting here now, healthy, happy, stable, successful people.
Nicky (1996)

I do feel pressure. More to become a replacement for Richey than anything, and I'm certainly not going to do that. We're not ever going to get another guitar player in, even though we could do with one. Mind you, they wouldn't exactly be queuing up for that one, would they? 'Guitar player required. Must mutilate himself on stage and carry impossible demands on shoulders for ever…'
Nicky (1996)

We've set up a trust fund so that all Richey's royalties go into this account under his name. If he ever turns up, he's got his share. That was really depressing going through all that legal shit. You've got to wait seven years until he's declared dead. We were signing all these forms, we wanted everything to be so proper, so if he ever turns up it's all there for him. But doing that, it just makes him seem like a number. It's really sad.
Nicky (1995)

Maybe one day we could use the lyrics Richey left behind, but we need to come to terms with what's in there. There's some good stuff in there… I know you can't get much bleaker than *The Holy Bible*… but after that we didn't think people were ready for songs about cutting the feet off ballerinas.
Nicky (1995)